Catherine & Barry:

I think this is the perfect new
millenium gift for the perfect
hosts at the Berkeley B&B ...
because it's about time the guests
started contributing something to
the always-meaningful B&B experience!

Thank you both for your support,
your wise counsel, your encouragement,
your generousity, your friendship,
your love ...

Happy New Millenium!

Love,

Singing for Your Supper

Also by Edith Hazard

Rising to the Occasion (with Wallace Pinfold)

Singing *for Your* Supper

Entertaining Ways to Be a Perfect Guest

EDITH HAZARD

Algonquin Books of Chapel Hill
1996

Published by
ALGONQUIN BOOKS OF CHAPEL HILL
Post Office Box 2225
Chapel Hill, North Carolina 27515-2225

a division of
WORKMAN PUBLISHING
708 Broadway
New York, New York 10003

LIBRARY OF CONGRESS
CATALOGING-IN-PUBLICATION DATA
Hazard, Edith.
Singing for your supper : entertaining ways
to be a perfect guest / Edith Hazard.
p.   cm.
ISBN 1-56512-090-6
1. Entertaining.   2. Amusements.   I. Title.
GV1471.H39   1996
793.2—dc20   96-12467
                                      CIP .

10   9   8   7   6   5   4   3

In memory of my father,
Charles Ware Blake Hazard
his timing, his magic, his music, his faith

A word of caution to the reader:

It is important to note that two or three amusements may not be for everyone. Headstands and cartwheels are not offered as a dare to the sedentary; drinking games are best left to those who have made plans to walk home. In short, prudent selections made from the table of contents will ensure a second slice of pie and smiles all around.

Contents

Contents

This little book could not have found its way into your hands without the considerable talent, support, and patience of James, Duncan, and Angus King and their wee sister, Caroline, Fiona Proudfoot, Stephen Bither, David Kew, James Satterthwaite, James Page, Edith and Charles Hazard, Ed Bradley, Alison and Jim Dodson, Robb Spivey, James E. P. Noyes, Mireille Bougloff, Dan Wright, Sonia Hodgkins, Elisabeth Scharlatt, Jennifer Rudolph-Walsh, Julia Knapp, Robert Rubin, and Suzanne Wagner. Please give them a round of applause.

By Way of Introduction:
A Little History

In an earlier time, before the opiate television had overcome sociability, the need for entertainment was met, for better or worse, by those who had gathered together. Cousin Joan would recite a poem, Aunt Rose would whistle, and Uncle Roscoe's concertina would wheeze. The Twins would present a magic show (which they promised they had practiced since the last time), and before you knew it, the hour was late. Back then, stories were considered absolutely essential to successful after-dinner talk. Lists were published annually for those poor souls who couldn't face another season without at least ten new *tableaux vivants* subjects (those costumed figures fixed in a familiar pose — *Washington Crossing the Delaware* or *American Gothic* or, as one nineteenth-century author suggested to liven up a dull evening, *The Temptation of St. Anthony*). Whether you were invited to attend a formal dinner or to join the family for a picnic in the country, you were expected to bring along a little something to amuse. A gathering without entertainment was like a meal without food. No hostess could conceive of such a thing. No guest would risk the consequences.

Even as the gracious invitation was being accepted, the

mental list-making began. "I just wore the black gown with jet beads, perhaps I can squeeze into the navy blue by next Saturday. And since the dinner is in honor of Sarah's birthday, I will recite something from her beloved Browning." Or, "Say, Harry, let's work up something for Uncle Charlie's retirement party. Aunt Sis has given me some great stories, along with a crumpled fedora and that huge overcoat from his closet—I think they're the same ones we used years ago. Remember that gag? You stood behind me and provided the gestures. . . . Oh, come on, we can do it again. We could do him dressing for the occasion, buttoning his shirt, tying a tie, combing his hair, taking a shot of courage—you know, the usual eye–hand coordinations without benefit of the eyes—all the while expounding upon his virtues and puffing up his past exploits in the privacy of his boudoir."

Today when someone calls to extend an invitation for dinner you may ask, "May I bring something?" assuming the answer will fall somewhere between "I was hoping for a bowl of that fabulous salsa, the one you make with bananas and chili peppers" (not too much effort for you) and "No, everything is all set" (which means a bottle of wine or a box of chocolates will do nicely, almost no effort at all). An offer to supplement the repast has mysteriously replaced the obligation to carry the evening. A "hostess gift" industry (complete with bottle-sized bags made of fine cloth or paper for the guest who can wrap things only if they are box-shaped) has blossomed in the fallow land once bursting with varieties of home amusements. Imagine if the hostess asked you to brush up your impersonations instead of bringing a salad, or to perform magic tricks rather than produce meringues (although these last two are arguably one and the same). Don't worry, she won't. It's simply no longer done. But why?

It may have something to do with time. The Victorians seemed to have had so much of it. While every generation tends to carry on traditions, that age embellished, embroidered, and elaborated in a concerted effort not only to amuse but to outdo. And when deemed proper, they did. Who could top Professor Hoffman's suggestions in his 1879 *Drawing Room Amusements and Evening Party Entertainments?* Charades required scenery and costumes, makeup and music. A tableau without a proper frame was passé ("Gilded filigree or black enamel? Such an improvement over last year's gauze curtain!"). Colored smoke enhanced magic tricks, fruit knives transformed after-dinner fruit into a veritable zoo . . . "Couldn't we raise a stage at the end of the parlor?" . . . the heights became dizzying. But eventually the practice fell off. Perhaps it was because competition drove the art of home amusements to a state of unattainable perfection. As mansions were divided into multiple apartments, the parlor-*cum*-theater diminished or disappeared. The audience for this sort of entertainment (to say nothing of the rehearsal teas) went the way of the upstairs maid. Expectations outgrew the drawing room and began to long for broader dimensions.

Later, when life found father trudging back from a long day at the office, the radio became the new wave of home amusement. Then mother began contributing to the household income and television rode the crest. To be fair, the blame for the demise of "party pieces" (as they were known in earlier times) does not rest solely with technology. True, our natural reticence to perform has been encouraged by these Hydras-in-boxes. But by now the reluctance to perform derives as much from a lack of experience as from a lack of expectation ("I've never done anything like this before"). Add to this the built-in twentieth-century phenomenon of billable time, which encourages you to calculate how much each minute of your life is worth, and it becomes even harder to devote hours to practice: a little voice, the one coming from over your left shoulder, keeps whispering to the sloth within, "When will you ever use this?"

The answer is, "Often." Perhaps a well-meaning great-uncle will put you in charge of entertainment at the family reunion, not only for those under sixteen but for Saturday's banquet as well. Or by some piece of bad luck you could be wedged with eight perfect strangers in an elevator car that is stuck between floors. Or maybe it's the annual talent show at the office (you were hoping for a raise), an emergency baby-sitting stint, the fourth consecutive unpaid cable bill, a twenty-two-hour car ride with his kids, a dare, a bet . . . there is no end to the potential duty-calls.

To revive home amusements is to recall a gift every guest once brought to the party, considered then as essential as a knife is to cutting or, in Tommy Tucker's case, as a wife to a wedding. You might start a trend. Who knows, you could lead a nation to reform. Along the way, some semblance of mastery will undoubtedly serve to bolster your self-esteem, confidence, and worth. And if that's not enough, remember: the smallest effort can banish the specter of the "same old coulda stayed at home" party, and genuine skill is welcomed all over the world. So, what do you have to lose by learning a card trick, or a little sleight of hand? How can you shy from charades? Now, more than ever before, you *should* try singing, especially if the reward is supper!

Singing for Your Supper

A PERFECT GUEST ARRIVES...

❖

An invitation arrives in the mail. "How delightful," you say, and look at the calendar to check the date before calling to accept. By the time you've dialed the number following the increasingly misunderstood letters *RSVP* (some think they mean "my unlisted number is," others swear they have something to do with the periodic table), you've conjured numerous expectations: other names on the guest list, an elaborate menu, an earthy caterer, surprise appearances known only as "and Friend." Oh, it can get juicy. Naturally, you don't explore any of this with your generous hostess (except perhaps to mention your severe allergy to shellfish). You are calling to accept, not to hedge or quiz (Mother says that's rude and she's right!). "Yes," you accept, in fact you are "really looking forward to it" and manage to confirm what you have read—"See you Saturday at seven."

A timely acceptance is the first item on the perfect guest's checklist, followed by a standard set of considerations, each with its own intriguing subsets. Clues to the question "What to wear?" may be found in the invitation: engraved = black-tie; E-mail = blue jeans; handmade invitations to a masquerade = more than a mask. The possibilities for "What to bring?"—besides your own splendidly turned-out self—

seem to increase as the formality falls off. Evening attire rarely means potluck. "How to get there on time?" "Who will tend the baby/walk the dog/water the plants?" and other basics are your lookout and honestly hold little interest for anyone else. They're a fact of life as a guest.

But the guest list . . . now that's worth a subset or two. You know the hosts and you have some idea of the occasion. A fiftieth wedding anniversary (recently added to the endangered species list) will gather familial faces of all ages. Marty's Sunday-afternoon hikes and homemade soups tend to be a mix of the acquainted and one or two newcomers. Now, the good guest will work through the mental checklist and spend an additional ten minutes with old photos in an effort to remember names and significant life events. The perfect guest will envision the party much as a Secret Service agent scans a filled auditorium. There could be trouble out there somewhere. Your job is to prevent it from happening. There are files kept on prominent protesters, and there is also a type, a personality, that may require the creation of a new file. Just as predictions are made by the agent, they are also made by the perfect guest. Uncle Henry will go on at dinner, but Uncle Henry goes on wherever he is; the Twins will scuffle in the hallway, but they won't be seated next to each other during the luncheon; Marty does favor people who knit, and you don't—knit, that is—which can make for awkward periods of nothing but clicking. Charged with keeping the peace, the agent packs some heat. Sensing the bore, the fuss, the pregnant pause, the perfect guest prepares a modest list of diversions.

Not that the hosts haven't considered the potential for disasters. Is there a host who is free from the haunting memory of a charred roast, an inadvertent and thus all the more shocking disclosure, an unforgettable accident? (Remember the time Cassey stole Father's electric razor and spent the evening shaving mink coats?) Of course they have considered the liabilities, and they've decided to carry on. They will prepare as best they can: the ice on the doorstep will be salted, the ice in the freezer will be adequate. In some respects, their responsibilities are a lot like those of a stage manager. The place is readied, the lights go down, and the house is filled with an audience and a handful of actors. A good guest understands the distinction, a perfect guest is ready with lines on cue.

So there you are, transforming the refrigerator carton into a dinosaur's body, what better time to rehearse a joke or two? Or, on your way to pick up some lamb's wool (to replace what you borrowed on the last hike), you try to recall the details of a recent story about a new homeopathic pharmacy that carries blue-green algae. If physical separation doesn't work with the Twins, you can try bringing them together with that string-through-the-ring trick (it could keep them busy most of the night). Whatever the glitch may be, you have done what you can not only to anticipate it but to prepare a pleasant detour as well.

And what are the cues again? The signals for when to go onstage and when to sit appreciatively in the audience? Some are fairly obvious. You've been invited to dine by an inveterate charades player, and as coffee is poured the first grumblings can be heard *sotto voce* ("I knew she'd make us play" . . . "I'm so bad at this game" . . . "Last time I cost the team ten minutes"). You catch the eye of your disappointed hostess and say, quite clearly, how you'd been hoping for a rematch and would she like you to round up some paper? That's the good-sport cue. There are others. The back door slams shut, the host excuses himself to rescue the fruit and cake from a pack of teens just back from the movies (and to ask where they plan to spend the rest of the evening . . . who's driving . . . whose car?). Everyone at the table can't help but overhear the ensuing conversation, but in order to catch every word, they must stop talking. You wonder aloud what film the boys might have seen and in the same breath ask if anyone has been to the 3-D version of *Wambats in Drag*. No one likes being caught red-eared, as it were, eavesdropping, and they will be grateful for your effort to distract. That's the etiquette cue. There's also the spoiler cue, which involves identifying the member of the party who needs to be entertained one-on-one so that everyone else can enjoy themselves. And the déjà vu cue: same old people, same old conversations, same "delicious" food . . . you've been there. Only by divulging a dark secret, a fantasy, or a completely off-the-wall observation can you hope to pry loose a kindred spirit whose enthusiasm or curiosity will lead others to hunger for something beyond the ordinary.

Then there's the dummy cue. It's taken from a different sort of group: one where *everyone* "doesn't know a soul." All conversation is abandoned for a close examination of shoes. (Are they wearing Walkmans?) The collective silence is excruciating. Your hosts have exhausted their supply of attractions (more food, more drink, surely they could get somebody something) and themselves in the process (it *seemed* like such an interesting group). You look across the room and pick a straight man . . . "You know, Hal, I was out of town last week at a bankers' convention, that's what I do, banking, and one of the workshops offered was called 'Changing Your Image.' Now what do you think that meant? [*Don't wait for an answer*] Tie-dyed dark gray and navy? Not at all. As soon as the room was filled and the doors were closed we were each given three tennis balls, told to roll up our sleeves and start juggling . . . could have heard a pin drop . . . and by the end of the hour . . ." And so your story or joke or patter for a magic trick goes. This cue category is the most difficult to prepare for, because the link between your act and their interests, or at least Hal's interests, must be pulled from a relative void. Making segues out of sows' ears . . . or something like that.

While many cues arise unexpectedly—and the perfect guest must always be on his toes—there are other cues that are "prearranged," as it were. The Lord of the Dance (Geoffrey Wood from two doors down) may invite you to his Winter Solstice Celebration; from time immemorial all guests have been expected to perform at it. Perhaps your hostess's children have been promised that you will show them one, but only one, magic trick in exchange for an early bedtime. Moonlighting with a ragtime band is no longer your secret and the hostess did ask *before* you accepted her invitation if you would play for her father (the dinner is in his honor and he just loves Scott Joplin). Expectations, bribes, requests are a direct commitment between guest and host with some tricky nuances. Will the act please one and bore twenty? Is everyone on his feet, desperate to be in bed by midnight, ready to go but for your effort to turn out a caricature of each guest? You don't want to renege on the promise to your hostess, yet offering a rain check may be the more prudent choice to make.

Too much work? Thought it was an invitation to have

fun? Well, it was. But these cues aren't heard amidst throngs of merrymakers. No, indeed, these are the stuff of social discontent, and a perfect guest wouldn't dream of allowing such distress to go unalleviated. Along with accepting an invitation comes a willingness, even a responsibility, to play the odds. Ten to one the guests will arrive ready for a high old time and you can reserve your trick for a future, less scintillating engagement. When it rolls around, take heart. The pleasure of presenting a polished piece while rescuing friends from a slow death will be (at least half) yours. To perform or not to perform? Either way, it's a win-win situation for the perfect guest.

BREAKING THE ICE

❖

You've been through the receiving line (it was a lovely wedding, beautiful bride) and everyone is milling about, waiting for a glass of champagne or some directive from the bridal consultant. The word is passed along that the official photos are taking just a bit longer than expected. It's a *temporary* lull, which means there is absolutely no need to snag the band's microphone for a little stand-up comedy routine. Using the time to peruse the place cards at your table, you find you are not familiar with a single name and you recognize the dilemma: to break the ice or to be frozen in it? 'Tis nobler not to suffer shyness, but to be well armed with a joke, a small trick, a silly stunt. Nothing elaborate, no bells and whistles, just a little something to take off the chill. Once the pleasantries have uncovered all pertinent information—"How long have you known the groom?" "Did you make the trip in one day?" "I haven't seen bell-bottoms like those since 1969!"—be ready to jump in . . . "Did you hear the one about the drive-thru wedding?"

Telling a Joke

It's not that you can't go to the local bookstore and find at least six volumes claiming to hold one hundred best jokes each. It's not that you don't laugh when you listen to a comedian, any more than it is a lapse of memory when you forget a punch line. Some people can read a joke, laugh at it, memorize it, and they still can't tell it. One dear friend always gives the punch line first and then is unable to remember the story line, which doesn't matter because she is laughing so hard her words are unintelligible. Weeping, rolling on the floor, she apologizes for messing up while positively killing herself with hysterical squeals. She's a friend, so she's forgiven.

Of course, there are some people who simply don't get jokes, and it rarely occurs to them to make one. They won't read this chapter, because they hold to the tenet that joke-telling is an innate skill, just after blinking, sneezing, and curling your toes when someone draws a line along the sole of your foot. Well, it's not genetic. Nor is the development of a sense of humor wholly determined by environment. If you grew up in a house full of jokers, short-sheeters, and raconteurs, you probably have all it takes to tell a good joke yourself. But a somber past doesn't preclude a hilarious present. So start practicing.

To begin, choose a joke you just heard and analyze it. What makes it funny? A savage twist? A witty reverse? An all-inclusive blow? The pace? The face? Stand in front of the bedroom mirror and see what you can do to duplicate the performance. Try it again. Is it still funny? Work on adaptations, changing the vocabulary, the victim's ID. Slow it down, speed it up. What works best? When you find it, think about going public.

But first, know your audience. They are looking to be amused, not offended. As the number of special interests has grown, the safe group of joke subjects has diminished. In an unfamiliar group, the best bet is to tell a joke about yourself; you can decide later whether or not you were insulted. In familiar groups (in chambers, at a bas mitzvah or backyard barbecue), you can usually find the common thread, just as birds of a flock find a feather. Material for inside jokes is relatively more obvious. Some people laugh when they watch a sitcom, some guffaw when they read, a sorry few miss all humor on a regular basis. So even if you restrict your joke-telling to one-on-one, remember, no matter what style you adopt, it's tough to hit 100 percent. Familiar and unfamiliar groups alike may be temporarily out of humor. Tragedy, for example, rightly demands a higher level of decorum, but the incorrigible may be unable to suppress an impudent quip. Occasionally, black humor is just what is needed to pull a group out of despair. But the risk is yours, so it had better be really funny.

If you are telling a joke by yourself, you are relying on memory and delivery. Timing is key. So is priming. You open it up with a line that sets the stage: "Did you hear the one about the . . ." "I heard a good one the other day . . ." It's a way of saying "Get ready to laugh" without saying it. Delivery has a lot to do with personal style. Deadpan expression, exaggerated imitations, gestures, sound effects . . . put in whatever works for you. And practice.

There are different types of jokes: the long joke that wears the audience down to a point where they are easy targets for blindsiding; the one-liner that arrives with lightning speed and either makes a direct hit or continues traveling right over the listeners' heads; the current affairs or easy target twist (the latter almost always in bad taste); the blonde jokes amongst blondes. And since there is no performance without an audience, there is a dependency, a temporary symbiosis. That may be why some comedians are more comfortable wit with a straight man who needs to have the joke explained (along with half the people in the room). Others mix wit with sight and sound, hoping to fire up at least one synapse per listener. Material and performers often match up: introverts are known for their one-liners, extroverts enjoy a little more time onstage.

No matter what type of joke or style you use, the most important part of the delivery is remembering your lines. Every time you hear "I heard a great joke the other day," there's a fifty-fifty chance the next breath will hold "I wish I could remember it." So does everyone else in the room. When people have known you longer, expectations will align with reality and disappointments won't be as severe. But if you'd like to avoid being known as someone who never remembers a joke (the next worst thing to a reputation for always being late or never picking up the tab), there is a solution. When you've just heard a joke, do what you can, once you've stopped holding your sides and are sure of bladder control, to make a one-sentence analysis of it: the subject, the action, the object. A cold, concise, black-and-white synopsis (with visuals if they help) stands a much better chance of being recalled at the watercooler the next morning. Yes, you could write it down. You could also stand in front of the full-length mirror in the bedroom and practice telling it out loud to yourself. Idle time is always well spent silently rehearsing lines, but do consider the surroundings. Commuters are often unnerved by a passenger who is laughing hysterically for no apparent reason; they may move to the next car and later report you. Church services, lecture halls, libraries, none of these are appropriate no matter how bored you are, mostly because it's so difficult to leave unobtrusively during a fit of laughter.

Let's say you have nothing to do on a Saturday afternoon. You and your current squeeze are going to a friend's house for dinner, but the rainy afternoon is unclaimed. You've perfected the waltz, all professional athletes are on strike, and the apartment is remarkably clean. Why don't the two of you practice telling a joke together? All you need is a large overcoat, glasses, a pipe or cigarette and lighter, a pamphlet or newspaper (whatever you find on the coffee table), a handkerchief, and maybe a piece of candy. One of you will wear the coat (at least over the shoulders) and tell the joke. The other person will stand directly behind, inside the coat, arms through the sleeves. Your props are in the coat pockets.

Say you are wearing the coat. You may open with a cordial "Good evening, Nancy, so good of you to invite me for dinner." (Your partner's hand will offer to shake hands.) "Oh, and hi Fred, I didn't see you way over in the corner with Julia." (Your partner gives a high, enthusiastic wave that is embarrassed into fingernail-biting, fussing with the tie, finally sinking into a coat pocket as you give a nervous laugh.) During the course of the delivery, you may announce a need to take off your hat or put on your glasses; you may wish for a cigarette and then settle for a piece of candy. The audience may be so enthralled by the difficulties you and your partner run into (this is slapstick at its homemade finest), they will have lost track of the joke. It's the perfect setup for a succinct punch line—or a cover in case you've forgotten it. Best of all, whether or not the evening's guests recognize your talent, the two of you will have spent some quality time together (and in very close quarters, no less). That hardly sounds like practice.

Reading a Palm

Some forms of entertainment require only a strong belief in one's ability to perform (a belief based on considerable practice and a good set of nerves). Standing on your head while reciting verse can begin to feel almost routine in the privacy of your own bedroom. Other entertainments require the same degree of confidence *plus* some physical assistance from one or two guests (a volunteer to tap a spoon on a glass when you need a C, a good-humored soul willing to subject his larger-than-life nose to a caricature). But when you come to the aid of a party with an offer to read a palm or two, you will need a third and most unusual ingredient. You may have all the self-confidence in the world, you may have willing volunteers, but palm-reading depends upon a crucial modicum of belief among the guests. Note who in the room acted as if you'd said, "I could practice open-heart surgery"; who cried, "Why wait until after dinner?"; who silently raised an eyebrow of interest. The reason? You should not read a reluctant palm, nor should you be discredited by one of Madame Vieux's regulars. Explain that you are merely an amateur. The fatalists and the neo-Gypsies will help you find a volunteer from the mildly interested group. "Go ahead, it

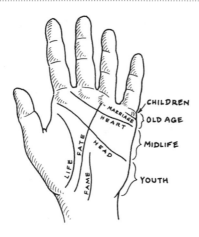

will be fun, and you don't have to believe anything he says because he's new at it."

That being the case, let's proceed to the practice round. If you are right-handed, begin by reading your left hand (to learn your original destiny) and then check with the right hand (to determine how just a few wrong turns made you drive right by that destiny). Lesson number one: palmists don't start with the palm, they start with the back of the hand. The shape of the hand, the length and spacing of fingers, the muscle tone, all are very much part of the reading.

There are four basic hand shapes. The "square" hand is just that: the palm is as wide as it is long, generally the fingertips are more square than round, as is the base of the palm, and the shape is considered to be the mark of a practical, energetic worker. A "pointed" hand, with its graceful almond shape and smooth skin, is the hand you see in Revlon's nail polish commercials, requiring oh so many hours of unqualified care. A "spatulate" hand becomes wider from the base to the fingertips, which are noticeably broader than the fingers, and most often belongs to an innovative albeit unconventional soul. A "cone-shaped" hand has a round palm and long, tapering fingers (the better to hold a brush, my dear, and to carry the spectrum of emotions ascribed to artists throughout the ages).

Straight fingers are an indication of strong personality traits; fingers that bend toward another finger reveal a weakness. The space between fingers has to do with just how generous (or stingy) you really are. Flexibility in the thumb is directly proportional to the flexibility of its owner. A firm, fleshy "mount" on the palm below the index finger is the sign of an open heart, while one below the middle finger tells of dark thoughts. A mount below the ring finger is found on hands with artistic potential, and one below the little finger has more to do with coping in general. The mount below the thumb gives you an idea of what could have been and what is in terms of sexual vitality. A corresponding mount above the wrist is indicative of creative imagination.

Enough already, you say. Tell me about my love life. Well, the heart line is the top line that runs across the palm, beginning just under the index or middle finger and ending at the side of the palm. The line below the heart line is the head line. If there is only one line running the width of the palm, it is said to be the head line (hearts will rule heads should the line be high, heads will cool hearts should the line be low). The life line starts just below the head line and curves down around the base of the thumb, ending above or at the wrist. Lines are telling in their depth, length, and continuity. Length is not as important as depth; breaks or islands indicate periods of loss. A fork at the beginning of the heart line indicates a loving nature, whereas a feathered beginning is the sign of a fickle heart. If the heart line runs close to the base of the index finger, you will have a fine marriage; if it touches the rings at the base of the index finger, the marriage is doomed.

Time for some wisdom handed down from professional fortune-tellers: the more palms you read, the more you believe. And the more you believe, the more you see in a palm. But you may not always see good news running along those lines. Think about ways to sugarcoat bad news, to find a strong positive to counter the negative (lucky in health if not in love, famous and wealthy despite a midlife crisis), and deliver them simultaneously. After all, you are a beginner and this is a party, and who's going to want to hear—to say nothing of believe—that you've just read the palm of an ax murderer? In fact, if you are presented with a palm that is absolutely loaded with breaks and chains and islands and crosses, you can fall back on your lack of experience with something like, "Wow, I've never seen a palm like yours, Jim, I need one that's a little easier to read. . . . Natalie, let me see that left hand of yours."

Natalie may want to know if her writing will make her famous, and her fiancé, Ned, wants to know if they will have children. The line of fame is one of two vertical lines running from the wrist to just below the base of the fingers. The line of fate is the other. If there is only one line, consider it to be the line of fate, and as for fame, well, the person whose palm you are reading (in this case, it's Natalie's) will have to be told that there is no need to worry about avoiding the paparazzi. If the line of fate crosses through the head line and touches the heart line, thus forming a large **M**, considerable good fortune is to be announced—lots of money, a good marriage—and if fate is doubled by the line of fame, it could mean a fabulous second marriage or two fortunes instead of just one. These vertical lines are divided chronologically by two horizontal lines—the area of youth lies between the wrist and the head line, midlife between head and heart, and old age above the heart. So while

Natalie is told that she will enjoy a very private public life, she can be encouraged to expect a fine marriage and possibly two. As for children, the answer can be found just below her little finger on the side of the palm, near the marriage line. It's actually easier to see the marriage line if the pinkie is bent forward. From the finger down to the marriage line there may be a number of vertical lines, one for each child. Ned may be astonished to hear the number seven, but he's the one who asked. Redirect his attention to the magic **M** and ask if they've played the lottery lately. Nothing to worry about, Ned.

Making a Rabbit or a Mouse

According to the calendar, it's supposed to be the first day of spring. Your hostess, who actually broke in mid-January and bolted for warmer climes, is back in town and giving a party in celebration of the promised thaw. You arrive, fifteen fashionable minutes past the hour, and enter what might be taken for a greenhouse or a very busy florist's shop the week before Easter. It's an overdone, indoor, forced spring of tulips, daffodils, narcissus, and grape hyacinth covering every horizontal space in what was, in fact still is, her living quarters. "How remarkable," you say, trying to take off your coat without falling into the herbaceous borders in the vestibule. And it is, but your remarks are undoubtedly best left unmade until there is time for polite editing. Especially since you can't help but feel as though you're on the set of *The Wizard of Oz* or *Alice in Wonderland* as you navigate through the foliage.

Offers to help have been declined, drinks and nibbles passed, and you find that no matter which threesome you approach, the conversation is mired in spring—the weather, the forecast, last winter, next winter—and *you* had been preparing a succinct analysis of the latest congressional hearings. In a corner, looking vaguely confused, is the hostess's Great-aunt Lucy, in need of cozy company. You oblige and lean toward her good ear. "Lovely party. Hasn't Bunny outdone herself this time?" Her nod could be more enthusiastic, and you realize this may be the only other guest on your wavelength, so you confide in her. "I think the only thing missing is some fauna."

With that, you pull the clean, white hankie from your pocket, shake it free from its folds, and proceed to drape it squarely over your right hand so that everything is evenly covered from the wrist forward. Using the thumb and middle finger of your left hand, push down along the sides of the right hand's middle finger, forcing the handkerchief to meet below the finger. Take the left front corner of the hankie (soon to become the left ear of the rabbit) and pull it around the outside of the thumb and up between the index and middle fingers; then take the right front corner and pull it around the outside of the pinkie and up between the ring and middle fingers. Voilà, you have two ears, a nose that twitches with the most subtle movement of the middle finger, and two cheeks. "I'd like you to meet a friend of mine," you whisper to the Lovely Lucy, and her face sheds thirty years. "My father used to do that trick for us," she sighs nostalgically, "and then he would make a little mouse that would jump onto my shoulder. Oh, he was such a dear, funny man . . . ," and her sparkling eyes begin to well up.

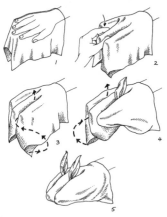

Making a Rabbit

No sooner has Aunt Lucy said this than you have shaken out the rabbit and spread out the handkerchief on the couch. Take the top right corner and bring it down to meet the bottom left corner. Now you should have two isosceles triangles, one on top of the other. Along the edge of the fold, pull the right point toward the center; then do the same with the left point (see the illustration). The points should overlap by an inch or two. Now the handkerchief has the outline of a standard frame house. Begin rolling from the foundation toward the top of the roof until the side triangles no longer show (that would be to the eaves). Pick up the hankie by the roll and change its shape from a log to a

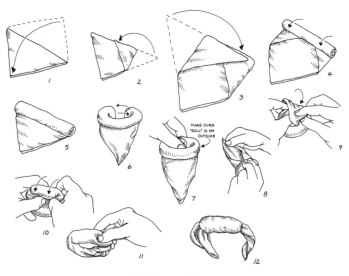

Making a Mouse

donut (the top triangle or roof should now hang from the middle of the circle). Now, pull the triangle up around the two joined ends of the roll and stuff it into the center of the ring. Keep on stuffing, unrolling the donut as you feed the triangle into the hole, until (miraculously) two corners of the hankie appear, looking like pointed ends. One of these corners will be the tail—choose the shorter of the two. The second corner should be flattened and rolled from the point of the corner toward the "body" of the mouse. This roll is a miniature version of the earlier log-to-donut roll. Take the ends of this roll and tie them together—the knot becomes the head, the ends are the ears.

Now, with Aunt Lucy seated on your left, gently hold the mouse in your left hand (resting the tail between the tips of your index and middle fingers and the head on your

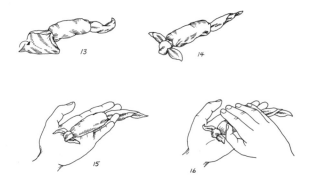

thumb). Cover the back end (and your fingers) with your right hand as you pat the mouse. With practice this takes less than a minute, and Aunt Lucy has waited forty-seven years to see this little white mouse again, so a few more seconds aren't going to matter to her. The mouse is trembling just a bit and you wonder aloud if it might jump. Invite Lucy to calm the little creature. She pats the mouse once or twice and then, with a quick (and imperceptible) flick of your left index and middle fingers, it jumps onto her shoulder. What a commotion! What a surprise! You have stolen Aunt Lucy's heart.

As for the other guests, their fascination with the weather was dissipated by a particularly intriguing tidbit about Harry Tisdale's distant cousin Raylene. The evening lurches on in fits and starts. At last the hour is acceptably late and Bunny is beginning to look for someone to initiate an exodus. You oblige, glance at your wristwatch, and mumble the tried-and-true "no idea of the time," offering to see yourself out with many, many thanks for a delightful evening. As you're leaving, Aunt Lucy takes your hand in both of hers and says she was charmed to meet you and that you must come again soon, before she leaves for Sarasota. "Harvey and I would like that very much," you say, pulling a small datebook out of your jacket pocket. "What night would be good?" Oh, to be twenty years older.

Hanging a Spoon

Upon occasion, may it be ever so rare, you might find yourself trapped in the snare of deference. Uncle George is pontificating. The dessert plates have been cleared, coffee has been poured, and still his voice drones on. Perhaps it is a family gathering. The table is ringed by faces that appear only once or twice a year, lending a peculiar time-lapse quality to the setting. And while Uncle George always has something interesting to say, your mind has wandered back to an earlier, unfinished conversation with Cousin Charlotte, a novice who has been awakened recently by her biological alarm clock. Time to look around the table for signs of breaking patience: fingers repeatedly tracing the pattern woven in the place mats, or glazed looks fixed just beyond the centerpiece. You watch the wrinkles build on Aunt Gracie's brow like so many storm clouds, mounting from mild resignation to marked exasperation. This is an opportunity to go beyond the duties of a good guest and take the bullet for Gracie and her company.

While conveying continued interest with a nod or polite half laugh–half sigh, gently push back your chair so as to be slightly behind your dinner partners. Slip your teaspoon off the table in an absentminded way. If anyone turns to watch, return your attention to George (unless, of course, it is someone who knows the trick and might be encouraged to support it with a knowing smile at the spoon). Holding the spoon vertically, touch its tip to your upper lip and exhale into the bowl. This can be done while you appear to be listening intently, as if you were unaware even for the slightest second that you are blowing into a spoon. Lower the spoon and wipe the condensation from the bowl. Return the spoon to your lips a second time. Exhale, fogging the bowl once again, while checking one last time on Uncle George's audience. Still entranced or completely spaced? Good. Now move the spoon from your lips to your nose, at about the point where it softens from bone into cartilage, and allow the bowl to rest on your face from that point down to the bulb. The condensation will make the spoon stick, which means that any placement involving a series of adjustments may dry the spoon and cause it to drop. (A closed lap will make for a quiet, unnoticed fall.) Knowing the exact point on your nose for spoon-hanging is critical, but fortunately easily learned through practice.

Remember, this stunt is most successful when it is least suspected. The last thing you want to do is call attention to yourself in the process. The entire operation, from the time you choose your weapon to the first giggle, should take less than three minutes. Even if everyone is desperate for some distraction, a series of false starts will simply elicit raised eyebrows of disapproval or, worse, a renewed effort to muster interest in Uncle's oration. But why carry the entire burden? Let the next person who ceases to find interest in her thumbnails—the one who is slowly raising her head to look about the room for a kindred soul—work with you. Technically it will be her uncontrollable laughter that ends the lecture.

If Uncle George has an ounce of good sportsmanship in him, he will get the message and join the others who are now trying to hang their spoons. It's such a simple trick, easily mastered and wonderfully ridiculous. Just the thing to relieve tensions and move the evening along. But while spoon-hanging works well as a lighthearted ambush, timing is everything. The test of a good guest is knowing when—and when not—to use it. Eventually, spoon-hanging may serve the family as a symbol for situations in need of a diving tackle. Just as *FHB* ("family hold back") is murmured from mother to ravenous child, and fingers are laid aside siblings' noses (last one to notice does the dishes), merely picking up a spoon and catching the eye of Sister Charlotte may do the trick.

Additional Icebreakers

AT THE TABLE

❖

There are many reasons why guests linger at the dinner table: not enough chairs in the living room, the dining room is warmer, the conversation defies interruption. Schematically, it may have something to do with the intimacy of playing "in the round." And yet most of the time leading up to this moment has been spent sating individual appetites. The focus has been on "Something more to drink?" or "Another serving of ratatouille?" not to mention "the most sinful chocolate cheesecake you've ever eaten." Yes, there have been exchanges here and there. Your dinner partner is an old friend and you manage to bring each other up to date on current events before you offer to clear for dessert. There is some back-and-forth with Jim and his new wife (she used to live in Houston and can't quite get over the snow ya'll have up here), but for the most part the activity has been eating and drinking and intimate tête-à-têtes.

Then, just as everyone is returning napkins to the table (the signal for intermission, the time when guests are most apt to consider whether to leave under false pretenses or to stay for the whole show), Alex reaches for an empty wine bottle and asks if the cork was saved. She drains the last drops into her glass and begins to tell the group about this most fantastic, truly awesome trick she saw the other night. The host retrieves the cork and hands it to Alex, who proceeds to force the somewhat swollen stopper back into the neck. "Pass this around the table and see if someone can get the cork down into the bottle without breaking either object." (This is a trick, but not the *real* trick.) "Once the cork is inside the bottle, I bet I can get it out, in one piece, without breaking the bottle, using only what is on the table." Now, who do you think is going to leave this party? One little puzzlement has opened what promises to be a fabulous second act. There's not an empty seat at the table.

How did Alex do it? Well, hold one corner of a napkin in your fist, between your thumb and index finger. Gently pull and twist the rest of the napkin with the other hand, making it narrow enough to fit into the neck of the bottle. Thread the napkin into the bottle, funnel-shaped end first, and then tip the bottle slightly, doing what you can to coax the cork to fall/roll/slide into the napkin (like a baby in a blanket). Keeping the bottle upside down, pull out the napkin. With perseverance, and considerable strength, the cork will come too!

Making Music

There was a time when music lessons served as a weekly reminder of how much you needed to practice before the recital. The daily list of "have yous?" invariably included "practiced for your music lesson?"—just after "fed your dog?" and "made your bed?" That the question was asked at all seemed somewhat ridiculous (unless the Steinway was in the conservatory over in the west wing); you assumed everyone could hear you play the same eight measures with the same seven mistakes over and over again. And yet because the question was asked with such regularity, it made the act of practicing oddly solitary. (Was *no one* listening? Didn't *anyone* care?)

On the long-awaited day, Mother would starch your collar and Father might even leave work a little early, but the performance was up to you. Lesson number one on the value of audience participation. Terror may have been eased by the sight of every relative you could name (including Frannie, a second cousin once removed), by beaming smiles and popping flashbulbs as you walked onto the stage. It might have been virtually eliminated when an older student flubbed a piece you played perfectly last year. And even if you yourself forgot an entire movement, family, friends, and fellow students would clap and say you had done a wonderful job.

Years later, though, you may find yourself before a very different audience. Perhaps you're visiting your sister and her family in their new brownstone. It's a dinner for several families: one is from the office, another is in the church choir, a third has two kids who go to school with your niece and nephew. Bitsy pipes up with "Did you know my Uncle Rob sings in a band?" The band is no big deal, really, just a group of friends who get together on Thursday nights to rehearse in case they get a gig. But Bitsy's boast of your musical prowess takes the conversation in a new direction ("Maybe after dinner you could sing us a song or two?") and you are presented with a choice: to carry the evening on your back or to share the load. Test the waters by expressing a few reservations (you need instruments, a backup chorus). If you are still at the table, and their interest seems genuine, why not give a brief demonstration of tuning glasses and ringing the rims of crystal goblets? Then you can think about adding a makeshift percussion section.

Begin by gathering some empty glasses, a spoon to tap each glass, and a pitcherful of water. Line up the glasses and fill them each an inch or so fuller than the one before (this may vary, depending on the height of the glasses). Ideally, you'd like to have eight "full" notes (that's tone, not water level) all lined up and ready to play. A purist in the crowd may ask for sharps and flats too . . . it is up to you to determine the degree of sophistication your audience requires. If the choir member guest is a recent conservatory graduate, you might want to turn the whole production over to her!

By decreasing or increasing the amount of water in a glass, a sharp or flat note can be resolved (more water produces a lower pitch). The range of a given glass may be only three notes, so you will need to find different types of glasses in order to cover the scale. Test the notes you have by playing a simple tune (tap gently!). "Mary Had a Little Lamb" will give you four notes for sure, "Twinkle, Twinkle Little Star" will fill in three more. The glass with the least amount of water should carry the same note as the glass with the most—but one octave above. If every member of the party takes a glass, you can try your hand at conducting (it does take some talent, as well as considerable concentration to translate faces into notes—Susan becomes C, Bitsy is E, Roger, G).

Crystal goblets filled with water in just the same way can also make music, but without being tapped. Simply hold the base of the goblet with one hand (it's important not to touch the stem) and begin tracing its mouth with the fingertips of your other hand. No noise? Dip your fingertips in water and try again. Perhaps you can convince Phillip to work that shrill pitch into the performance for a twentieth-century effect.

Blowing straight across the top of a narrow-necked bottle will also produce a musical note. In fact, during some idle hour of your youth, you might have learned to get *more* than one note from a bottle. Maybe it was a day back in junior high school when you and your brother were waiting for a ride home after the game. You'd finished your Coke and couldn't figure out what to do with the bottle. So you blew *across* the opening and then you blew *into* the opening. And two different notes (actually, it's the same note in two different registers) blared out across the parking lot. At a party, if eight guests line up with eight bottles filled at intervals, just as you did with the glasses, you could have a pretty good wind section. A perfectionist would insist on precisely tuning the bottles (by adding just the right amount of water), but for a more relaxed crowd the bottle section can work for the bass line, the percussion solo, or a mean combo of the two.

If your adorable sister served jug wine for dinner, or the recycling bin holds a special place for heavy plastic containers, an empty jug can be used as a bass (or is that *base?*) instrument. Unlike a bottle with its straight path of air blown across the top, a jug is played by making what's known as a raspberry into its mouth. It's a little like spitting (the tongue protrudes) and a lot like a rude noise, but as you adjust the tension of your bottom lip, the sound varies and resonates with the jug. You can actually play any tune on a jug if you work at it. But don't assign this instrument to a shy dinner guest—and be sure to provide a towel.

Finally there are the spoons, the ultimate music-at-the-table instrument. Take two spoons of similar size in your right hand (assuming you are right-handed) and hold them together, back to back, with your index finger between the bottoms of the handles. Your thumb and middle finger keep the spoons aligned. Alternate hitting the bowls down on your knee and then up against the palm of your left hand. Like everything else, with a little practice, you (or your impromptu band members) will be able to maintain a rhythm and perhaps even add a few impressive flourishes. Among the glasses, goblets, bottles, jugs, and spoons, you and your fellow dinner guests can work out quite a routine. Add some lyrics, some doo-woppa-doos, and lots of practice and you might even consider going on the stage (Sis says one leaves in ten minutes).

Composing a Limerick

Most reunions are held together by stories, be they deliciously fresh or dismally hackneyed. For the most part, these tales have to do with an earlier time. A time of innocence and immortality, introspection and irreverence. Cousins, schoolmates, former neighbors join the familiar chorus, "Remember the time when?" which is followed by gales of laughter and cries for more. "You remember the time Mary and I showed up at your house driving her grandfather's brand-new car? You know, it was that two-toned green Plymouth with push buttons instead of a stick shift and we could barely see over the dashboard. It was when we were in sixth grade." Grandparents claim ignorance, parents take the Fifth, and children learn that the funny stories rarely make mention of being caught.

Being a guest at someone else's reunion can be something of a challenge. These are not your memories, and while the variations on the themes of close calls and pranks can be amusing, they begin to slide beyond the category of Predictable and into Deadly Dull. You might be tantalized by the camaraderie and begin telling tales from your own remarkable past. Or you might be tempted to make a few surreptitious notes on other guests. If you suspect this reunion scenario is in your otherwise splendid future, you might consider the limerick, a most generous little device. While it entertains the masses, it can also serve as a tonic for the bored and alienated. It may be offered in the form of a toast, as an inscription, or as an after-dinner remark.

True, these rhymes are most often known for their ribaldry. Many's the barmaid who has turned a deaf ear to an endless evening of recitation. One avid sportsman claims to hold a standing invitation to fish or hunt anywhere in the world based solely on his store of limericks. But the fun of a limerick should not be confined to the lodge, nor should the would-be limerick perpetrator remain content with merely memorizing some other pundit's wit. The formula is accessible to all and it is not essential to take the low road. The higher plain may not bring crude guffaws, but innuendo, euphemism, and double entendre remain the true measure of a memorable limerick. (NOTE: Subtlety will make your composition twice appreciated at intergenerational gatherings when parents of young children are asked to explain why everyone is laughing so hard. "I'll tell you later, darling . . . in the car . . . on the way home.")

There are three basic elements of the limerick to keep in mind. The first is the story line, the second is the rhythm, and the third is the rhyme. Let's say you are at Fred's reunion and his best friend, Lance, is introduced to you as the man who had uncommon taste in clothes and women. You would like to know the story behind the introduction and start to wonder if his mother was a cross-dresser (okay, you're *very* bored). The rest of the gathering looks like molasses in January, so why not work on a limerick? Begin by dividing your story into five stages: (1) introduction of the main character, Fred; (2) introduction of the second character, Lance, and the relationship between the two—politics and women; (3) their dilemma—lusting after Shirley—and their interaction—she receives invitations from both Fred and Lance; (4) the climax of the interaction—she accepts both; and (5) the conclusion or moral of the story. Each of the stages is given a single line, making for a total of five lines per limerick. Altogether it could sound like this:

> College chums Fred and Lance did believe
> Marx was right, "We must share to be freed"
> The rub was discovered
> While sharing a lover:
> Virgin Shirley elicited greed.

Before you decide on a story line there are a few more technical points to consider. Rhythmically, there are nine beats in the first, second, and fifth lines. The accent (the heavier beat) falls on the third, sixth, and ninth beats in each of those lines (it sounds something like dada DUM, dada DUM, dada DUM, and is formally recognized as trochaic hexameter). Lines three and four are shorter in length and have only six beats, with accents falling on the third and sixth. From beginning to end, then, the rhythm of the limerick sounds like this (go ahead, say it aloud, clap it out, do what it takes to imprint the pattern):

> dada DUM, dada DUM, dada DEE
> dada DUM, dada DUM, dada DEE
> dada DUM, dada DOO
> dada DUM, dada DOO
> dada DUM, dada DUM, dada DEE

As you will note, lines one, two, and five need to end with the same rhyme (*way, say, day; believe, deceive, conceive; Turnbury, real scary, how dare he*). Lines three and four, the couplet if you will, share a second rhyme (*shade, laid; bare, share; thigh, deny*). There may no longer be a standard for this sort of composition, but if there were, you would receive additional points for reaching beyond the "ings," "ays," and "ees" when choosing your rhyme scheme. To delight and instruct, the following limerick is offered:

> There was a young Scot named McAmiter
> Who bragged of excessive diameter
> Yet it wasn't the size
> That opened their eyes
> But the rhythm—trochaic hexameter.

Brevity continues to be recognized as the soul of wit, but true wit so rarely makes an appearance these days. The limerick embodies both brevity and wit and is thus well worth the effort. Composing a limerick on the spot is the mark of a pro, and there's no reason why you can't become one. As an absolute beginner you might go to the library and read, even try to memorize, numerous limerick collections (you may begin to get an ear—to say nothing of an earful from the humorless librarian). As an amateur, you might set some time aside the day or two before an event to consider the angles and players, develop a story, and tease it into a verse for just the right moment. (Be prepared, the moment may not arise, in which case you will have to write down the limerick and mail it to the alumni magazine.) Once you're an expert, you will be able to eavesdrop during the afternoon activities, shuffle characters and rhyme schemes to a point of satisfaction, and offer the limerick just as the photographer is disappearing beneath the black focusing cloth.

Performing a Magic Trick

Magic is as varied as its beholders, from the young believer to the weathered rationalist. Some of the purest magic plays so often in our daily lives it usually goes unnoticed. Consider the egg. Would you believe that this fragile structure could withstand the impact of a drop from a second-story window onto a grassy lawn? No? Then that should be your first magic trick. Go to the refrigerator, take out an egg, go upstairs, and open a window overlooking the lawn. Give the egg a gentle, believing toss and watch it fall without fault or fracture to safety below. That's magic. (Unfortunately, it's magic that works only on lawns, so don't choose a window over the driveway.)

Now, take the same egg to the table. (Actually, the egg may be a bit scrambled inside, so it might be best to use a second egg.) Can you or any member of your party make the egg stand on its end unaided? Let everyone have a try and then ask them to go into the next room for a moment while you enlist the services of a magic spirit. As soon as they are clear of the doorway, pour a small mound of salt onto the table, no more than half a teaspoon (frugal and superstitious spirits may be watching). Nestle the larger end of the egg into the mount, rotating it slightly to form a supporting crater in the salt. Without touching the egg again, gently blow the excess salt away from the base. In this case, "excess" means all but five or six grains, which will be imperceptible to even the sharpest eye. When the guests reenter the dining room, it will appear that you have succeeded where others have failed.

Another form of magic substitutes sleight of hand for the wonders of nature. This kind of magic makes rabbits pop out of hats to nibble on the bouquet inside a newspaper. It involves hours of practice, clever patter, steady nerves, and the occasional use of phenomenal paraphernalia to make things seem to be what they are not. Books and catalogues abound for magician's supplies—and packets of chemicals for colored smoke, pitchers with linings, and altered card decks can certainly result in an impressive show—but that kind of show is decidedly more appropriate for the stage, or for a party where you have been booked as the entertainment, not invited as a guest. An invitation to dinner is just that, an invitation to dinner. Unless specifically requested, arriving with a black cape, top hat, and wand would be presumptuous at best. On the other hand, everyone needs a little magic from time to time. And should the occasion arise, why not be prepared to provide it?

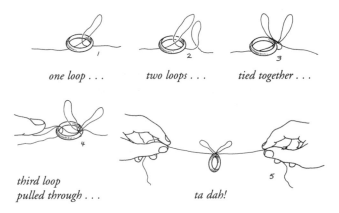

one loop . . . *two loops . . .* *tied together . . .*

*third loop
pulled through . . .* *ta dah!*

This is a trick that calls for a piece of string, a napkin or handkerchief or other similar covering, and a ring. With the exception of the string (which fits easily into your pocket before you leave your house or can be borrowed from someone's shoe), the props can all be found at the table. The type of ring you need is a simple band, nothing ornate, no Tiffany settings for this trick, just a plain ring (the heavier the better). A napkin of paper or cloth, a handkerchief, a dish towel, even a paper towel will do. Your practice sessions should involve a variety of rings, strings, and coverings so that you know how these variables factor into the act.

You are about to thread a string through a ring while the two ends are being held by other people. If you can work this action into the after-dinner discussion (perhaps as an analogy to the Middle East peace process or to congressional attempts to balance the budget), all to the good. If not, have a story ready to frame it. It could be the story of the ingenious Aretha. "There are two important figures in Aretha's life: the film producer, Jane Albatross, her boss of twelve years to whom she has become indispensable, and her fiancé, James Hart, who is currently an overqualified and underemployed director of *ciné noir*. Ms. Albatross and Mr. Hart share an interest in Aretha's time and her future. Neither is willing to make fewer demands. Aretha is feeling unmercifully pulled in two directions at once." (You can embellish this tug-of-war triangle or develop another story altogether. The more complexities you enlist—that is, the more distraction you provide—the more miraculous your trick will appear.)

You have noticed a wedding band on the hand of your dinner partner and he seems to be an easygoing sort, so you turn to him and ask if you might borrow his ring just to make a point. Of course, if his wife shoots him a "you promised you'd never take that off" look from across the table, be ready with a second choice. Assure the lender that the ring's disappearance (which may be the unspoken desire of several people at the table) is not part of your act. When obtained, put the ring on the table in front of you and place the string just below it in a straight line stretching to the right and left. Invite everyone to look at the string and the ring ("You see, there's nothing irregular about either object"). As you put a napkin or other covering over the ring and center part of the string, explain that you, acting as the clever Aretha, will be able to get the string through the ring while both ends are being held. Since the tightly reined man on your left wasn't allowed to lend his ring, ask if he would mind holding one end of the string. Ask the person on your right if he would mind doing the same. Eye contact is important, not only with the two volunteers but with the rest of the audience as well. To prove once again that there are no gimmicks, uncover the ring and string . . . "You see, they remain apart." Then cover them for a second time and continue with your story. "Aretha goes to the gym with her girlfriend to get rid of some tension." You put your hands *under* the napkin. "She says she has no intention of either quitting her terrific job or leaving the love of her life, but somehow she needs to get both parties to lighten up, for goodness sake." Explain to your volunteers that you may need a little slack, but whatever they do, they should not let go of their ends. Using the center of the string, make a loop and *put it through the ring* (see the illustration). Then, using the string just to the right of the ring, make a second loop and tie the two loops together in a fairly tight over-and-under fashion, like the first step in tying your shoes. While you are doing all of this, continue with the story . . . you left off in the middle of a conversation between Aretha and her friend: "These two are ruining what should be the happiest time in Aretha's life. If only she could get them to appreciate each other, or just to respect each other's needs . . ." and so on. If this is a party of social workers, lawyers, mediation consultants, or the like, you can either bring their buzzwords into the story or go outside their realm—Aretha's friend could be an astrologist, anxious to know everyone's sign. In the meantime, don't forget you are in the middle of a trick. Using the left side of the string, pull a third loop up through the ring and hold that loop with your left index finger. Remember, your hands are under the napkin. You can practice the trick up to this stage by tying knots with your eyes closed, but at some point you will need to incorporate the napkin into the act, as the unveiling plays a crucial part.

Thank both volunteers for their help, gently taking the end of the string from the man on your right while continuing with the story. "Aretha has found a solution. She has written a script that cries out for the genius of Mr. Hart's direction and the reputation of Ms. Albatross's production." Remember, don't take your left hand out from under the napkin; the finger holding the third loop must remain on the table. Begin pulling the string from the right (not with a sharp jerking motion, but more as if you were shifting to assume responsibility for holding the right end). Turn and nod a silent "ditto" to the volunteer on your left. If he doesn't get it, thank him again and ask him to let go. As soon as the left end of the string is under the napkin, pull the loop through the ring and grasp the end, all while you are flipping over the napkin to uncover the mystery. What? Are you lost? Go back to the part where you make the third loop. Your left index finger is pressing the third loop to the table; now you take the right end of the string in your right hand. Okay so far? Start pulling the entire apparatus slowly to the right, so that when the left end is released by the volunteer it is about to disappear under the napkin. As soon as the left end has traveled into the third loop, grab the end and bring your hands out from under the napkin. Now you should be holding both ends of the string and the ring should appear to be tied up in a bow. "So, you see, Mr. Hart and Ms. Albatross have become entwined."

Skeptics will quickly jump in. "You didn't say anything about tying the string to the ring, you said you could get the string through the ring. . . . I can tie a bow . . . any fool can do that." At this point, if you have managed to do every-thing correctly, you should be able to pull both ends of the string and stun the nonbelievers. Calmly reply, "You are right, I did say I could get the string through the ring. That's the beauty of this story, because while Mr. Hart and Ms. Albatross have become engaged in a mutual interest, Aretha is free to move between them." Then pull both ends of the string straight apart as quickly as you can; the knot will dis-appear and the ring will spin around the taught string. "Magic!"

Some serious practice is essential for this trick. The tying, the pulling of one end as you slip the loop and catch the other end, all while unveiling the ring, can't take too much time. It needs to be done quickly and as smoothly as the telling of the story, and all while you are encouraging eye contact with the two volunteers and the crowd (get them to take their eyes off the table just for an instant and you're home free). Once you have mastered this trick, you may not want to share its intricacies, particularly if it's the only one you've got. Simply smile, return the ring to its spellbound owner, put the string in your pocket, and ask if there is any more of that delicious decaf.

Producing Shadow Puppets

According to the credits before and after most films, making a motion picture involves veritable legions of multitalented, card-carrying folks. For every person who appears on camera, there must be twenty tweaking this and brushing that behind the scenes. Who do you think clears out all those locations at four in the morning? And what wizard conjures up the computer magic that makes just the right amount of light fade at just the right time? Moving pictures have come a long way indeed since the days of their primitive ancestor, the shadow puppet show, which employed just one individual to serve as actor/director/producer and required no more than a cave wall, the light from a blazing fire, and some idle time (say, just before opening day of the mastodon season). At that time, the artist may have received only a grunt of appreciation. But if you were to take up this ancient art today, you'd be likely to win rounds of applause (or, should any members of the party be under the age of ten, attentive adoration for the rest of the evening). You need nothing more than the Neanderthal did, although lamp- or candle-light may be more appropriate against a dining room wall than the light of your precocious predecessor's open fire.

Start by standing with your back to the light and stretching both arms out toward your right, parallel to the floor. Most shadow puppets are produced with your hands (unless you have a long cape and are going for "Tales of the Monster Bat") . . . try to put as much distance as possible between your torso and your fingertips. In keeping with the ominous

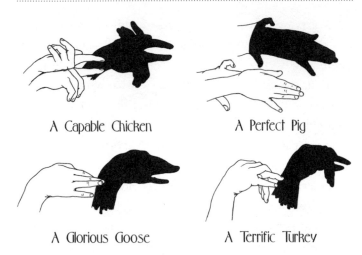

A Capable Chicken

A Perfect Pig

A Glorious Goose

A Terrific Turkey

nature of shadows, you might decide to strike a blow for vegetarians by bringing the main course back to life. Pork chops, pâté de foie gras, or the holiday drumstick: all are easily recalled. The script and voice-over are up to you. If you think "The Ghost of Tom Turkey" will ruin little Sarah's finicky appetite, review the story line of "The Little Red Hen." When all else fails, just ask "What do you think this is?" and be prepared to lend an encouraging squeal, honk, or gobble.

A Capable Chicken

Hold your left hand out, palm facing up, thumb following along the index finger, which is straight, forming the eye and the top of the beak. The left middle, ring, and little fingers are folded into your palm, the knuckles serving as the comb on top of the chicken's head. Now, put the back of your right hand underneath the left so that the backs of both hands are touching. The middle, ring, and little fingers of your right hand point to the floor to form the wattle (that's the proper name for that nasty-looking wrinkled bit of skin that flaps and shakes when the chicken cackles and clucks), and the right index finger extends to form the bottom of the beak. If this shadow puts you in mind of a novice contortionist you once saw on Channel 76, you are probably doing it correctly.

A Perfect Pig

Your left hand forms the tail and one hind leg of the pig and is otherwise hidden behind the right. The thumb on the right hand is the pig's ear. The palms of both hands are facing the wall, the base of the right hand resting just beyond the knuckles of the left. Adjust for anatomical accuracy by gauging the appropriate distance between the pig's tail (left pinkie) and its ear (right thumb). The three middle fingers of the right hand are tight together to form the piggy's thick neck, forehead, and protruding snout (overlap the fingers slightly to keep any stream of light from shining through — you want a solid black piggy, not a Gloucester Old Spot). So far, so good. A quick review: curl and wiggle the piggy's tail by bending the left pinkie up and down. The left thumb is holding up the rear, as it were. The right thumb can move ever so slightly at the ding of a slop pail or the buzz of a fly. But what about that front leg? Well, this can't all be easy. Stretch that little finger of your right hand out as far as you possibly can (try to make it parallel to the left thumb—otherwise this porker is in a permanent nosedive). Having trouble? Call the pig to supper ("Sooey") and look at those legs run! (Bend and rotate your left thumb and right pinkie while moving the pig across the wall.) Now that's some pig.

A Glorious Goose

This is a one-handed puppet, which means you could initiate a gaggle to go with the goose and the gander . . . helpful little hands make very good goslings. Your right hand is held horizontally, palm toward the wall. The little finger moves up and down to close and open the beak. The index and middle fingers are tiered behind the ring finger, and the first joint of the thumb gently slopes at an angle to form the crown of the head. Your wrist and arm become the neck of this creature. Geese combine a waddle with a strut, ducking furtively for a bit of grain or hissing with a beak wide open and rushing at an intruder while all the goslings climb over one another looking for safety.

A Terrific Turkey

With palms overlapping and the back of the left hand facing the wall, use the index finger of the left hand to form the top of the beak. The middle, ring, and little fingers of the left hand drop ninety degrees toward the heel of the palm, drooping down to form the turkey's wattle. There should be no light showing between those three fingers, as the wattle is a single flap of skin. The left thumb blends into the line of the index finger. Now, the right hand (its back to the light) drapes over the left (picture if you will two hands resting on the top of a post or a walking stick). The knuckle of the right thumb forms the crown of the head, the first knuckles of the index, middle, and ring fingers become the face. Think of the bald head of this Tom. These four digits should form a continuous, rolling contour of wrinkles. Here's the key: rest the ring finger against the left index finger (remember, it's the top of the beak) and the right pinkie easily becomes the bottom of the beak. Open and close, open and close . . . you are clever. Now, do what you can to tidy up the head and beak, hiding an errant thumb or straying finger. Flutter the wattle and give it your best gobble. Not as easy as it sounds? Oh, come on, you still have enough time to get this down before Thanksgiving.

More Food for the Table

DRAWING ROOM ENTERTAINMENTS

❖

What is the difference between the life of the party and a crashing bore? The answer is: a fine line. It's the very same line that differentiates appropriate language from vulgarities and proper attire from go-go boots. The trouble is, it's so fine you can't actually see it. You have to intuit it starting at a fairly early age. To be sure, there are guides along the way to let you know you've crossed it. A raised eyebrow, a whispered reprimand, and when you're "old enough to know better," an offer to be driven home.

Compounding this problem of invisibility, the line also wavers according to the company you keep. If you stick with a crowd of World War II vets, you can't know enough Cole Porter. If you hang out with scalawags, your vocabulary won't ever seem base. If you bask on a nudist beach, you'll never be too anything. But when you find yourself in an unfamiliar group or in one that is made up of varying ages and persuasions, that fine line begins to wiggle all over the place. The hour, the libations . . . too much of a wavy line can give anyone a headache. Call for a bromide.

The Golden Rule usually works well to ease the confusion, as does a loose translation of that line from Ecclesiastes—"There is a time and a place for everything" (which is usually followed by "And this is neither the time nor the place"). This second rule requires a high degree of objectivity (or someone standing over your shoulder). When all else fails, consult the oracle. Ask yourself, "Will this seem like a good idea tomorrow?" and then look around the room. Reciting a bawdy limerick, telling an off-color joke, suggesting a rambunctious round of Thumper, it all fits within *your* definition of good fun, but probably it would be best to wait . . . at least until the children have been tucked into bed.

Reciting a Poem

Long ago, it took twelve days to celebrate a holiday properly. The pudding had to be cured for at least three weeks, the house needed cleaning before decorations went up. There were clothes to lay out, gifts to wrap, cards to write, and, well, the lists went on forever. Now we give a holiday forty hours, between the time stores close on the Eve of and when they reopen for returns on the Day After. We may attribute the shift to demands for a higher GNP or to secularism masquerading as inclusiveness. Either way, it shows a great deal about how Americans, citizens in the land of labor-saving devices, do less with more time.

The same may be true of the art of recitation. It was once a part of the daily classroom routine; today it's no more than an extra-credit option offered once every other year. It seems to have fallen from fashion with the rise of free expression. (Why memorize what someone else has already written when you could be spending the same amount of time unfettered in free verse?) And then there is the issue of pertinence. How relevant is the language of the Bard to the grade school student of the twentieth century? If it is of no interest to the pupils, why should it be required? Prevailing wisdom is often like a prevailing wind. It can shift.

One day, when the pendulum swings back toward twelve-day holidays, restoring those customs will be a simple matter of research and marketing. But reestablishing the merits of recitation may be less easy, since the atrophy is likely more severe. It is possible that aid could come from an unlikely quarter: the cultural reverence for supple, taut, immortal Youth. No one argues with the proponents of physical exercise or with the substitution of fiber for fat. Everyone at some time becomes engaged in the search for soul (in machines, music, or mankind). All that's left is a willingness to "round off" the picture with some mental gymnastics. Reenter the recitation of poetry.

Most poetry written between 1360 and 1920 adhered to a list of rules honed, honored, and handed down from who knows where. Poetry's success was measured against strict guidelines for meter, sound, and sense. Schoolchildren who endlessly analyzed the classic poems grew into adults who could appreciate the intricacies and nuances of a new work. In the way a moderator employs *Robert's Rules of Order* and fans follow a football match, the activity was contained within a predetermined structure. For reasons left for others to debate, the rules surrounding poetry and recitation may need a brief review.

Meter is the number and pattern of heavy and light beats in a line. In fifth grade you probably spent some time putting slash marks between words marked with curves (unemphasized) and apostrophes (emphasized). Having trouble recalling the process? Take a look at the first four lines of Andrew Marvell's "To His Coy Mistress":

Had we but world enough, and time,
This coyness, Lady, were no crime.
We would sit down, and think which way
To walk, and pass our long love's day.

Do what you can to determine a consistent rhythm. Yes, each rhythm has its own name; they have probably comingled in your "things I never fully learned" drawer along with types of columns, protozoans, and Latin conjugations. The vocabulary, the poetese—dactylic hexameter, iambic pentameter—will be left for another time. The object here is to be aware of the number of syllables and the emphasis given to each one. In each of Marvell's lines there are four "feet";

each foot consists of a light beat followed by an accented beat . . . ta DUM, ta DUM, ta DUM, ta DUM. Clap it out, mark it up, do whatever it takes to understand the meter:

Had we / but world / enough, / and time,
This coy/ness, La/dy, were / no crime.
We would / sit down, / and think / which way
To walk, / and pass / our long / love's day.

Sound can be a rhyming pattern linking the ends of lines; it can be a hard or soft sound made by a letter that is repeated throughout the line; it can be the enunciation and expression suggested by a word (*Wow!*). Sources of sound weave a pattern that sometimes follows the meter but more often threads its way in and around the beat.

Sense. What's the message? It's all well and good to stress the rhythm while highlighting the patterns of sound, but what is the author trying to say? There must be a reason for the poem's fame, but at first glance it may not be too clear. Read it to yourself as if it were prose. Read it again for meter, and a third time to find repeating sounds. Use an accent (British, Brooklyn), use an attitude (lascivious, weary). Take heart, the effort may serve you thrice. Once to enhance delivery (nothing like understanding what you are saying when you're trying to hold a crowd), a second time to facilitate memorization, and finally to provide for some amusement. In identifying the words that rhyme, the syllables within a foot, the progression of thought, you have inevitably become more familiar with the text.

The struggle to "scan" a poem is almost as helpful for memorization as learning the melodic line of a song. (NOTE: It has been shown that some poems work easily into a familiar melody when committing to memory—Dickinson's "Because I Could Not Stop for Death" sung to the tune of "The Yellow Rose of Texas," Frost's "Stopping by Woods on a Snowy Evening" to "Hernando's Hideaway," a rapper's delivery of Chaucer's general prologue from *The Canterbury Tales*. The incongruity, not to mention the irreverence, is distracting, but go ahead and give it a try if you like.) You can practice your piece almost any time. An hour or so with mirrors and privacy is helpful once you get to the stage of thinking you have all the words, but while you are working up to that, any period of empty time will do. While waiting for the next train, make a list of the last word in every line. Picture one word per line and give it some action or connection to a key word in the next line, and so on, creating a chain of visuals. Repetition is the most straightforward approach to memorization. Saying the poem over and over and over, silently and aloud, will get you there every time (thinking it is good; saying it and hearing it are even better).

Now that you've identified the components of your poem

and employed a few tricks to hold it in your mind, it's time for the recitation. The performance, if you will, be it given as a toast, a profession of love, or an after-dinner party piece, is not unlike patting your head, rubbing your stomach, and trying to blow a bubble all at the same time—only a bit more difficult. Don't be lured off course by singsong or lean too heavily on the meaning. Reciting poetry is a kind of mental juggling; three or more pieces of equal weight are connected in one fluid motion. While you are taking a good, cleansing breath, think of the elements—the meter, the sound, the sense—and how you have worked to keep them together.

As you climb into this well-conceived chariot, ready to be transformed from retiring guest to flawless performer, make one last safety check. Nothing stops the flow quite as surely as a sharply raised eyebrow. Before you begin, remember: the selection of poetry is almost entirely personal, making it twice as easy to commit to memory. At the same time, it is unlikely that you will undertake such a feat without an audience or an occasion in mind. If a dinner conversation leads you to believe that your choice might offend, begin with an apology couched in historical references, a brief profile of the poet, one or two definitions to clarify archaic language, even why you wish to recite the poem despite the potential faux pas: "I have heard this poem read most convincingly by a woman who took great liberties with intonations and furthered the case against philanderers." Or, "Words have a tendency to fall in and out of the gutter, regardless of when they were actually written down. We are left with the choice of constantly editing collections of poetry or overlooking a current (and possibly lower) meaning in order to appreciate the beauty intended."

Enough said. The poem, please. Give it your heart and you're bound to win at least one in return.

Playing Dictionary

"Every language has its anomalies, which though inconvenient . . . must be tolerated among the imperfections of human things . . . but every language has likewise its improprieties and absurdities, which it is the duty of the lexicographer to correct or proscribe." So reads a very small portion of the preface to *A Dictionary of the English Language*, compiled by that "slave of science, the pioneer of literature, doomed only to remove rubbish and clear obstructions from the paths through which Learning and Genius press forward to conquest and glory, without bestowing a smile on the humble drudge that facilitates their progress," the lexicographer Samuel Johnson.

All work and no play certainly made for a prolific curmudgeon. But suppose Dr. Johnson had put a spin on his efforts and found a way to twist his onerous task into more of a lark. Oh, if only he and Boswell had stumbled onto a game of Dictionary when they first set off for the Highlands. Well, they didn't, but you can. All you need is an articulate group of players, a dictionary (the more complete the better . . . if your library includes a compact *OED*, and the players are champion weight lifters, this would be the time to use it), slips of paper, and enough pencils for the entire group. While you are waiting for everyone to settle in, pass the dictionary (or gather around it) so anyone who wishes can refresh his memory of its format and style. Most dictionary entries begin with the word itself, followed by the pronunciation and alternatives, the part of speech (noun, verb, adjective, and so forth), and the derivation (Lat, Fr, Gr). Then the definitions are given, sometimes elucidated by a synonym or a sentence using the word. If this is entirely new information to any of the players, you might do well to choose another game. In other circumstances, though, especially if the hour is late, this review may improve the game.

Once everyone is ready to start, one player, let's say his name is Charles, chooses a word from the dictionary that, in his humble estimation, is notable for its obscurity. The word is announced. If Julia knows the word, she must disqualify herself from the round. Only players honestly claiming ignorance can qualify. (At this point, Dr. Johnson rolls over.)

The object of the game is to write a definition of the chosen word that is so structurally sound and linguistically convincing that it will receive the most votes from the other players for being the correct definition. (This is how Julia's knowledge could be turned to her unfair advantage and why it must be nipped in the bud.)

Charles has chosen the word *leguleian*. He announces his choice (with no clues other than the correct spelling) and writes the dictionary's definition on a slip of paper: "of or pertaining to petty questions of law or to law language." Then there is a period of silence while everyone furrows their brows and stares at their blank slips.

Katrina writes down her definition of *leguleian*:

n. also: *leguleianne.* archaic. 1. A term used in the Middle Ages to describe a diet of roots and tubers followed by certain European religious orders. 2. One who follows such a diet.

Noah submits:

Leguleian: one who sees all events in relationship to the law. A fixation with the legal system.

James counters with:

Leguleian: (EC. Af.), A member of the nomadic Legule tribe of Kenyan herdsmen. 2. A distinctive pattern of repeating arrow-shaped designs found on artifacts from this region.

Mireille writes:

Leguleian: adj. (Fr. gul) foolish in nature, gullible.

All definitions are turned over to Charles, who arranges them, along with the real definition, in an interesting order and labels them by letter or number. Without divulging the author's name, he then reads each definition aloud slowly and deliberately to the would-be lexicographers. No laughing. No nodding toward the author. Whoever is "it," in this case Charles, must give each definition audible credence, otherwise the vote will be skewed toward the definition that is read without giggles. Someone may ask to have a definition repeated. Another may need to hear all five of them again. As soon as decisions have been reached, the voting begins. Charles asks, "Is it A, gullible?; B, medieval diet of roots?; C, legal fetishist?; D, African tribe?; E, petty questions of the law?"

Katrina votes for A, James votes for B, Noah for E, Mireille for C, and here's how Charles tallies the score. If a player votes for a wrong definition, its author gets a point. Thus, Katrina receives one point for James's vote (he actually thought her definition was the right one), and Mireille gets a point from Katrina's vote. Noah earns five points for choosing the correct definition, the one from the dictionary.

(If it hadn't been for Noah, Charles would have received two points for stumping the lot!) Charles then passes the score sheet and dictionary to the person sitting on his left. Let's see, that would be James, who chooses the word *jink*. It's a new find he was keeping for Scrabble.

Singing a Song

Washing the car on a bright, sunny Sunday afternoon, zipping along the treadmill at the health club, driving four cherubic ballerinas to their weekly dance lesson, you absentmindedly sing along with the radio. Your teenage son is aghast, your car pool is amazed, you admit to being on automatic. Signs of a misspent youth? Perhaps. But ten to one, if your U.S. history teacher had set summaries of the week's reading to the tune of "Jailhouse Rock" or "Runaround Sue," you'd still remember the names of the seven generals, the dates of the battles, and something about the outcome. Nothing like a melodic line to recall the lyrics—whether you liked them or not—from the dark reaches of your mind. A melodic line *and* the opportunity to hear the song over and over again—community sings, summer camp, grade school chorus—that is how the old chestnuts were kept warm. Where else would you have learned the words to "I've Been Workin' on the Railroad," "This Land Is Your Land," and "The Erie Canal"?

Some wonderfully talented woman who could play the piano from a standing position while directing a group of twenty-eight rambunctious sixth-graders replete with crackling tenors and tittering sopranos did what she could to explain basic harmony and how to breathe using your diaphragm. And every week the same five songs were rehearsed. Singing was a group activity, meeting the 100 percent participation expectation of the teacher and the ubiquitous vice principal. There was a decided safety in numbers. No single voice was great, but by concert time the whole group was surprisingly good. Occasionally, one student would be chosen to work on a slightly more complicated piece of music for the graduation exercises. "Good luck" was whispered in a strange mixture of envy and relief. For nine of every ten chorus members, the burden of a solo performance was material for a recurring nightmare. You may have been in that majority, and yet this morning, thirty years later, you are singing in the shower with complete abandon.

"But that's not me singing for an audience; I'm by myself with perfect acoustics," you protest. The idea of a solo performance remains right up there with root canals and midflight turbulence. Don't worry, many people will give the same short emphatic "NO" to the question "Do you sing?" Does this fear stem from the trauma of public humiliation experienced during a nursery school spring concert? Were you asked to lip-synch in chorus? Is it an inexplicably high standard shared worldwide, that if you open your mouth to sing you'd better be Pavarotti? Excuses for not singing may be specific ("I can never remember the words") or overly general ("I can't sing"). Sometimes they are a combination of the two. While lyrics can be reproduced and handed out, courage is more difficult to come by. Lessons require practice, practice enhances rehearsals, rehearsals build confidence, and confidence instills courage. So, stand up straight, feet eight to ten inches apart, toes pointing slightly outward for balance, hands on hips. Take a deep breath and then slide your fingers forward to rest on top of your abdomen. Start panting, not by expanding and contracting your lungs, but by pushing in and out with the muscles of your abdomen. If your fingers don't move in and out, you aren't using your diaphragm. "Who cares?" you ask. Anyone who needs to hold a note or get to the end of a line without expiring, is the answer.

Run through a scale (eight steps up and then back down) using *la* for each note. Next try "Do, re, mi, fa, sol, la ti, do." When this gets boring, mix it up. Sing the first note of the scale (we'll say it's middle C), then its third (E), then another third up (G), and then to the top of the octave (C) and back down through G and E to middle C. Now use the same progression one note up from C, that would be D. D, F, A, D,

A, F, D. Chances are you don't have a pitch pipe in the shower. The note you start with may not be C, but for this exercise it doesn't matter one whit. Think of this as stretching before a long run or after an endless drive. How do the neck and throat feel? A bit tense? Do what you can to relax them. As soon as you are warmed up, choose a song that you first sang around the age of five (suggestions: "Twinkle, Twinkle Little Star," "Frère Jacques," "Did You Ever See a Lassie?") and sing it in a comfortable key, not for the benefit of an accompanist but to minimize any strain on your voice. In other words, if you can't easily cover the lowest note, or hit the highest, start over in a higher or lower register. How did it sound? Not bad or a bit rusty? Sing it several more times. Play with it, give it a variety of syncopations: first it's a march, then it's a country-western number. Now that your rendition of "Twinkle, Twinkle Little Star" has grown so sophisticated, you might want to pick up the lyrics to an adult song you like and try it out with the same gusto you gave to your childhood favorite. Chances are you've heard the song played many times, so you're familiar with the melody and the beat. All you need to do is read the words.

Remember: Along with being dry and fully clothed, there is another significant difference between singing solo in the shower and giving a performance in your neighbor's living room. The acoustics simply aren't as tight. In most situations, it would be unrealistic to expect to find a portable microphone lying around, so with the exception of lullabies, give your full voice to the song. Projection is a combination of posture and confidence, and the result is a voice you never knew you had.

Also, it's time to start memorizing those clever lyrics. It's fine to practice with the sheet music in hand, but lining your overcoat with "fake books" is excessive. What is the story or message in the song? Visualize the action. Select four or five crucial verbs or subjects and list the rhyming words in sequence. Whatever trick you devise to retain the lyrics, remember that the melody will also act as a kind of safety net. A sequence of notes often provides the clue you need to pull those words out in time to sing them. Of course, the surest foundation is to sing the song over and over again, for days or even weeks, until you switch on to automatic . . . remembering the words becomes no more difficult than remembering your name.

Thanks to all this practicing, your voice is limber, your breathing is controlled, and you have begun to play with the song—singing faster and then very slowly, using a heavy accent, adding a flourish with a mouth trumpet or whistle. It's yours to enjoy, and at some point you might begin to believe it could be for others' pleasure as well.

Now that you have a solo piece, think about how you might encourage audience participation. The pleasure of your newly won success is reason enough to proselytize. To convert a collection of diners into an a cappella ensemble is to hand out duplicate keys to a long-locked door. Depending on how musical you perceive the group to be, you could suggest singing a round. Start with the most familiar ("Row, Row, Row Your Boat" will do) and work toward something with a bit more flair, such as "Scotland's Burning." Just to make sure everyone knows the tune and the words, sing it through one time in unison. Get everyone to stand, take a deep breath, and sing it again. Now, break into two or three groups (depending on the length of the song and the total number of singers) and be prepared to act as director in case there is a shy group. If necessary, rearrange the groups to spread the wealth of willing and able voices.

This does begin to sound like a fine time, particularly the bit about getting everybody involved. All it takes is one brave soul to overcome the universal fear of not measuring up to Ezio Penza or Lena Horne; a ready list of classics (that is, songs most everyone has heard that do not include an instrumental bridge and rarely require the range of a soprano or bass); and two or three wonderfully daring friends.

...

Playing a Drinking Game

It has been said that families who pray together stay together. Or was it families who *play* together stay together? Heaven knows, there is a bond formed in collective rowdiness, whether inside or outside the home: when a junior choir is laid waste by antics, when mothers leave their young to join other mothers on a weekend spree, when fathers and sons vie in end-of-season soccer games. Even among strangers — remember waiting for the freshman trip bus with that nervous group of would-be backpackers? And if all the players are over twenty-one and have relinquished car keys and pitched their tents, rowdiness *may* involve imbibing. So without further ado (or judgment), here are two drinking games that are on the record as being both rowdy and companionable in nature.

Thumper is a game of signals for at least five but not more than ten players. Each player needs a glass and an adequate source of resupply (what you drink is your decision, but beer is the usual beverage of choice). Each player also needs a sign — Jerry's is his right index finger against the right side of his nose, June's is a wink of her left eye. And so it goes around the table. Everyone should know who has what signal. The object is to repeat your signal as soon as it is given and then give another player's signal to pass the action along — that's two signals per pass. Signals must be made in full view, that is, it's unfair to turn away from the person whose signal you are giving. On the other hand, it's completely within the rules to be very quick with a response, to return the action of the player who just passed it to you, to speed up a rapid duel and then throw in the sign of the least attentive member of the group.

The first round is started by the person who suggested playing Thumper; in this case that would be Chuck. All hands begin drumming on the table. Above the din, Chuck asks, "What's the name of the game?" and the crowd answers "Thumper," at which point the drumming and all talk cease. Chuck pulls his left ear and then puts his finger alongside his nose, passing the action to Jerry. Jerry must immediately put his finger to his nose and then wink with his left eye if he wants to turn things over to June, or make Junior Birdman goggles, a personal favorite, for Kate, who returns the goggles and then pulls her left ear. Chuck is busy watching June and misses the signal. Everyone points at Chuck, not with their fingers (that would be rude) but with their elbows. This means a penalty for Chuck, who must take a sip of his beer. Penalties also go to anyone who points incorrectly or talks during play. Since he missed his signal, Chuck begins the next round—all players drumming—by asking, once again, "What's the name of the game?" and, hearing "Thumper," signing in and over. After five rounds everyone stops to adopt a new signal.

The Prince of Wales is to Thumper what a doctoral thesis is to an undergraduate term paper. As in Thumper, the optimal number of players is between five and ten. But unlike the silent, physical game of Thumper, the Prince of Wales is a verbal exchange of accusations and denials. One player is designated the Prince of Wales and all the others count off, starting with the player to the left of the Prince. The Prince declares that "the Prince of Wales has lost his tails and doesn't know where to find them" and then calls out a number—let's say it's three. The accused number three replies, "Not I, sir," and the Prince asks, "Now who then, sir?" at which point the accused becomes the Prince and everyone's number changes, with number one sitting to the left of the player who started out as number three and is now the Prince. The new Prince calls out a number and waits to hear "Not I, sir" before countering with "Now who then, sir?" and assuming a new number. The game is to be played with considerable speed. Denials may be shortened from "Not I, sir" to "Nice" and queries from "Now who then, sir?" to "Whose?" Just to mix things up, the Prince may call out "Reverse" before a number, which means the order switches from clockwise to counterclockwise, or back to clockwise, depending on which way you were going before the reverse was made.

Penalties are accrued by players who respond out of turn

("I thought *I* was three, when did I get to be *seven*?") and by players accused of being too slow to respond (the question of fairness may go to a higher court, and should those at the table concur that the response was not so slow after all, the player who made the accusation must accept a penalty for an overly hasty reproach). And if a player responds too quickly (that is, if she calls out a new number *before* the Prince has time to ask "Whose?"), a penalty is also awarded. A penalty is usually a sip of beer or some other drink, but if you are tee-totalers (or underage), it might be a penny or a check mark.

No one need accept a penalty until the mistake is pointed out (with elbows, according to the etiquette of drinking games, not with fingers or voices). So don't say anything like "Oh, I forgot to count." Just hope that everyone else is too busy trying to remember numbers to notice or care.

To solidify the bond among players, there are "sympathy rounds": for a very good round (one that lasts more than five minutes would qualify), for an unbelievably bad round (when the second Prince forgets his lines), or when everyone in the group looks dry.

If anyone needs to be excused during the game (it is a good idea to hold phone calls and have easy access to a bathroom), a formal request is made after a penalty is given. The player says, "In but out," meaning, "Count me in even if I'm not here, I'll be right back." (NOTE: It is wise to resume your seat only after a new Prince is identified; otherwise you'll never figure out your new number.) The player who has had enough says, "Out but out," and is either replaced by another player or is no longer included in the numerical sequence.

Watch out for veterans of this game, especially those wearing purple. Some graduates leave their alma mater with a secret handshake, others bid farewell with a mind filled with logarithms. But this band of quick wits can spout the sequence of denial, question, and response more rapidly than their fathers could give name, rank, and serial number.

Entertaining Alternatives for the Drawing Room

FAMILY ENTERTAINMENTS

❖

You've been invited to a midday birthday party for Grandfather Csnezky. So has your mother, your brother, and all manner of kin. It's likely to be hours of varied interactions. A telling exchange with your sister-in-law, a warm embrace and reminiscence with Pa, listening to all that your nephew has been doing over the summer. Children seem to be everywhere, noisy, bouncing, racing through the house. Here and there you spot a loner. Someone out of sorts, feeling left out or simply misunderstood. Right before your eyes is that eight-year-old hope of the future disguised as a social misfit. What he's lacking is just what is needed to insure the family's heritage long after Grandpa C has departed. This child is an empty basket waiting to be filled with the stories and tricks and games and music that have made you so rich. So signal to that waif and go scout out two pencils and some paper. Return to the table with promises of secret magic so powerful he'll never feel left out again. Then quickly draw a caricature of Granny. Show it to your adopted wallflower. Does he know who it is? Does he have any suggestions about who else you should draw? Does he want to learn how to do it? Has he ever noticed his mother's ears? Pretty soon you'll have a table full of budding cartoonists. This is the grass-roots approach to home amusements, the only way the movement can hope to grow. You've got to start when they're little green blades.

Drawing a Caricature

Leave it to a three-year-old to wonder aloud, "Why does that man have such a big nose?" You squeeze your child's hand to the threshold of pain and begin a soulful account of the origins of hurt feelings. For better or worse, Shopping Mall Morality Lessons tend to have a lasting, even a chilling, effect on our powers of observation, or at least on our willingness to share those observations. Surely everyone can see that the woman is bald or the man has left his fly unzipped, but with maturity comes the ability to look beyond the glaring feature. That is, unless you are particularly paranoid, constantly imagining yourself giving a detailed description of every passerby to the police sketch artist. Or, better still, unless you are regularly commissioned to produce caricatures (one of the fortunate few who are paid to notice, nay, accentuate those physical features we try all our lives to hide). The freckles, the braces, the glasses thicker than Coke-bottle bottoms, the jowls, the mole, the receding hairline—they're all fair game for the cartoonist.

But why should cartoonists have all the fun? Why should a permit to make visual roasts, often for sizable rewards, be issued to so few? No doubt the answer has something to do with artistic ability, and even more to do with never having given it a try. Think of it this way: if you do give it a go, you might discover an innate ability to draw and be spurred on to higher forms of artistic rendering. Yes, you could be sent to the depths of confirmation that you have not the slightest bit of talent, but that despair will only increase your appreciation for those who possess the skill. It's a win-win situation, and with practice thrown into the can-do mix, just think how lively the deadliest Sunday dinner could become. The two aunties and that mischievous cousin Jack are perfect subjects. So, consider a basic drawing lesson.

Start by taking a different look at whatever you see. No matter what you choose, the object or scene will be made up of lines, curves, and circles (not necessarily the perfectly symmetrical type). Some are empty—the frames of the glasses—and some are filled—the iris and the pupil. Look at a truck from the side: three parallel horizontal lines, five vertical lines, four circles, and two curves. Now look at the tree next to the truck. Thin curves, thicker curves, one fat line, and an irregular circle. Get a blank piece of paper (raiding the "clean white paper bin" is admirable, and if your home office doesn't have one, well, that's for you and your conscience to wrestle with) and a pencil or pen. Do what you can to put those shapes you've just identified on the paper in the same pattern. So what if it looks like something a second-grader would be embarrassed to bring home? This is as private as private lessons come. You are the only one who will see your work, there are no grades, no jury or show at the end of the year. It's for your own enlightenment, to satisfy a nagging curiosity. Maybe this is something you could have been doing all along. Give it a try. Give it several tries.

From the primitive to the surreal, there is a reassuring array of legitimate interpretations. Caricatures lean more toward early childhood drawings, stick figures with definite cartoon qualities. In fact, the last thing you want is a caricature so portraitlike, so easily mistaken for a photograph, that the grotesque obliterates all humor. That's not funny, that's just homely Uncle George. The whole idea of a caricature is to accent the most prominent features (including personality traits). Remember those weird mirrors in the fun house? The ones that made you look like a pear or a beanpole? You laughed then, at least everyone around you did, so why wouldn't a portrait of distortion be just as funny today? Stop whining. You don't know you can't draw a face, you've never really tried. Close the door, find a photograph of someone's face—models in cosmetics advertisements are perfect—and give it a go.

Practicing with old magazines is recommended for a variety of reasons. It's private, it's unhurried, and it's two-dimensional. Look at the shapes of the head on the page and do what you can to break them down into straight lines, curves, circles, and angles. If you can't see the shapes, start tracing over the photograph with a magic marker, following only the most basic lines. Now, stand back from the photograph and concentrate on the lines you've made. Try to make the same ones on a blank sheet of paper.

The ear is a good place to start. It is somewhat isolated from the face and can be considered a separate entity. And during the preadolescent years, when time was impossible to waste and mirrors were brutally honest confidantes, ears gained in significance from "how I hear" to "how I look." Shape, size, and angle determined the choice of haircuts, earrings, and hats. Oddly, this universal familiarity (some might say fetish) rarely translates into an artistic rendering. Henry knows exactly how big his ears are. Monica may decorate hers with four rings per lobe. Mortimer wouldn't dream of ordering cauliflower from a waitress. Three for three can't draw facsimiles of this prominent feature only because they haven't tried.

You may gain a new appreciation for your least favorite body part after deconstruction. There is a large C curve that joins at its bottom to the lobe, a smaller c that may or may not attach directly to the jaw. The curve is generally a thick line, which can also be defined by two thin lines. From a slightly different angle, the curves almost form a lowercase **g** bumping up against the side of the head. By using a standard figure (the letter **c** or **g**, half of a figure eight, or whatever your imagination comes up with), you can begin to stretch the proportions to mirror—or better yet, to exaggerate—the size and shape of the ear.

Expanding on the first exercise, consider the shape of the entire head. Is it round, triangular, rectangular? Don't confuse outline with general features. The outline is what you would see if the head were reduced to a shadow. Draw it and then divide it into fourths (see the illustration) if your ren-

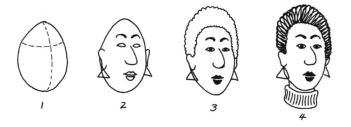

dition is made from a straight-on position or into sixths if the subject is busy talking a mile a minute to someone on her left (four parts for the right side of the face, two parts for the left). The grid will be erased later, but for now it's an easy way to get some sort of placement for the features. Eyes go along the horizontal line on either side of the vertical mark, the nose follows down the vertical, the bridge begins just above the intersection of the two lines.

How big are the eyes? How round are the cheeks? Are you looking at Bucky Beaver or Old Bushy Brow himself? What about the hair? Everyone worries about what to do with it, and what to do without it. But unlike most noses, hair can be styled and restyled on a whim. Color (be it a secret shared only with the hairdresser or an all-too-obvious shock of red, purple, or green), cut, and care given to a coif are like so many tea leaves when you are reading personality profiles. The safety here is that the statement is made for you; all you have to do is play it up. The same goes for jewelry, beards, glasses frames, and glittery eye shadow.

Selecting the prominent features isn't difficult, especially if you think of them in terms of how you would describe a person whose name you can't remember. Drawing those features may be more of a challenge. Repeat the magazine-photo exercise, but this time highlight one of the features. Make the eyes bigger or the nose more pointed, add some earrings and a toupee. If you're having trouble imagining the exaggerated lines, study your reflection in a lightbulb or a Christmas tree ornament. Look again at the eyes. What shape do they have? Are the corners even or is one more elevated? What about bags or crow's-feet or heavy eyebrows? What about the mouth? Is the bottom lip full? Is the chin double? How many lines appear with a smile? Are they curved or straight, deep or fine? Choose only the strongest ones, as a caricature works within the same principle as true wit. One or two insightful, well-drawn observations is all you will need.

Picture this. You and your old college roommate and her three-year-old (the sitter canceled at the last minute) are meeting for lunch downtown. Dutifully, the child has quietly observed all in the first ten minutes. Understandably, she is now having trouble sitting still. The waitress is doing what she can to coordinate the order (trying to have the hamburger without ketchup arrive with your appetizers), but the child is restless. "If you sit still for about five minutes, I'll draw a picture of you." Words of magic. Rearrange her hair, make her ears flap, measure the length of her nose, ask what color she thinks her eyes are. Does she know how to wink? Remind her you can't draw if she doesn't stop wiggling. And when the portrait is complete, allow her to be the first critic. If she likes it, and the breadbasket and curls of butter have yet to be replaced with real food, tell her to choose another subject. Maybe the lady at the next table, the one dressed all in purple ("Did you see her nails?"), or the maître d' who smiles broadly despite the unfortunate gap between his two front teeth. Soon the little girl is busily making her own drawings and her mother is eternally grateful. She now appreciates you as more than a friend . . . in her eyes you are also the perfect guest.

Cutting a Silhouette

Who can resist a pair of scissors? Not the blunt-nosed, painfully small, rough-handled sort issued to kindergartners, but the elegant silver pair used to clip a bunch of grapes, the efficient orange-handled pair used to cut fabric, the sturdy spring-loaded pair that hangs by the kitchen sink. These are the scissors that beg to be used. Slip them into your hand and you can't stop yourself from hunting for something, anything, that might need a trim. Many is the child who has fashioned her own haircut, sheared his grandmother's mink, fringed the sofa's slipcover. The scissors made them do it. And if the punishment was made to fit the crime, they were taught to be constructive with scissors. Lessons started with paper chains, progressed to paper dolls, and may even have reached the art of silhouettes. In school you used to make chains to hang on the Christmas tree. Your teacher probably asked you to fold a standard sheet of red construction paper while Jimmy cut up the green ones: first in half, then in fourths, and finally in eighths. The creases were guides for cutting strips that would be pasted together. (Ehew! Remember the smell of that white, gookey stuff?) Of course, the paste was lumpy and sometimes it smushed out from the seam and onto the link, but it was primary art.

Cutting paper dolls is rather more demanding. These are not the type found in magazine racks, the dolls of current cinema stars whose vast wardrobes are attached by frustrating paper tabs. No, no, these are a continuous string of dolls, carefully cut out to remain attached to one another, rather like the Rockettes. And they don't have to be dolls. You could choose dogs, horses, majorettes, or cowboy hats. Whatever your fancy, though, the outline must touch both sides of the allotted space. You'll see. Start with a strip of paper. Legal size is ideal, and for practice who cares if it's yellow with green lines? The strip should be 14" x 4¼". Fold the strip to make five even sections (they'll be just under three inches wide), alternating the folds from left to right in a fanlike manner. Think of an accordion, or a jack-in-the-box: the folds are in and out. The strip should now measure four inches by almost three, stacked five deep. Draw your figure of choice on the top piece. Remember to extend the design to both sides (hands and feet, tail and nose, baton and boot will serve as the connecting points). Then get out those trusty shears and cut along the outline, making sure you DON'T cut where the pieces will hinge together. Pick up the top doll and watch the other four unfold. This is the utmost fun for a young child and it will increase your appreciation for the art of paper cutting, but it may not work at a state dinner. Back to the cutting board.

Playing to a more mature crowd has its advantages. They remember with great fondness the hallway gallery of silhouettes at the old homestead, the annual session with Mrs. Grey, who must have snipped portraits for every family in the county, and they'd be happy to sit while you try your hand. Of course, you can admit to your amateur standing. They'll understand. After all these years, they had assumed it was a lost art. But that doesn't mean you haven't been practicing (or that their eyes are any less critical). The technique of cutting a silhouette is based on a keen ability to reduce a three-dimensional object to two dimensions. It's as if you can see the person seated before you in photograph form and reduce that form to a smaller size. There are two ways to practice. The first calls for a discarded magazine. The second requires a live model. Let's start with the first.

Look for a picture of a model in profile—the standard side view sort used in police lineups across the land. Put a blank piece of paper behind the picture and cut both sheets along the outline of the profile. The hairdo, the forehead, the nose, mouth, and chin . . . that's what counts. Never mind her beautiful green eyes, her splash of freckles, her dimpled smile—this is a silhouette. Now take the blank sheet and tape it to a background of contrasting color. You should spend some time noting the features that are distinctive (the slope of the nose, the crown of curls, the eyelid and lashes) or peculiar (the lantern jaw, the high cheekbones, the receding hairline). The smallest detail may be the most revealing. Just as the sidewalk portrait artist can pick up the nasty habit of recycling boilerplate features, silhouette artists have been known to give the same nose to every member of a family. It takes a practiced eye to note the prominent feature in an outline. The good news is you can practice anywhere. Silhouettes can be of houses, skylines, animals, and bedsteads. Look at the commuter who is staring out the window, or study the posters over his head.

Eventually you should try to cut a silhouette of a live subject. Ask someone to sit for you, someone who has time, is interested in the project, and isn't particularly vain. Your niece Lindsay would be a perfect choice. Besides this neat kid, you will need a table, a lamp with a cord long enough to reach two or three feet from the willing subject, and a piece of paper (yesterday's newspaper will do, it's just a practice session, remember?) to tape up on the wall. Lindsay should be seated between the wall and the lamp. Dim the other lights in the room, allowing the lamp to be the strongest source of light in order to produce the sharpest shadow. Ask Lindsay to turn to the side and hold as still as she can while you trace the outline of her profile's shadow, now projected onto the newspaper. When you finish, take the paper down from the wall (be careful not to pull a layer of paint with it). Cut along the line you have drawn. There you have a silhouette. It may be crude but it's a beginning. They will become more refined as you go along.

The final step in perfecting your technique is to eliminate taping the paper to the wall and tracing the shadow's outline. What? How are you supposed to cut without a line to follow? Don't panic, you can do it. Using the same sweet model, the same light, the same wall . . . it's nothing you haven't done before. Think of an actor throwing aside the script or a musician closing the score. If you want to start with the nape of the neck (because it's easier), ask Lindsay to turn her right side to the wall. Close one eye. Hold a piece of paper up to the left of the shadow and begin cutting what you see. Up the neck, around the back of the head, to the crown. At this point it may be easier to ask her to change sides, in which case you will turn the paper around and cut the front view—from the neck, up and out for the chin, in for the mouth, up and out for the nose, and so on, all the way past the forehead and up to meet the crown. No, it's not easy. No one ever said it would be. But if you think of the scissors as a sort of pen, you are actually drawing the outline with the blade. So practice, and then take a break. Practice some more and then take a shorter break. And after every reasonable facsimile, break out a smaller piece of paper (you're eventually hoping for something that will fit inside a 5" x 7" frame). If you've faithfully gone through the steps, you will begin seeing improvement. And just to be sure you do, save your first effort for comparison's sake.

A word about scissors: A good pair is essential to cutting a silhouette. In this case, good equals sharp. If you should be given a dull pair by your well-meaning host (and you'll know as the first cut pulls and tears the paper apart), retreat to the paper doll primitives, where the disadvantages of dullness are more easily concealed.

Playing with Cards

Forty years ago, it was widely rumored that census takers were instructed to ask how many members of a household played bridge. The card game was more than a national pas-time, it was a cultural preoccupation, from college lounges to convalescent homes. Evenings were built around the game. Syndicated columnists, cartoonists, and even manufacturers (all those card tables and tally sheets!) joined to celebrate bridge as the long-awaited successor to whist and pinochle. Handsome monogrammed playing cards (the perfect gift for any occasion) could be found in the drawer of every end table. Not that bridge was the only card game played. Poker

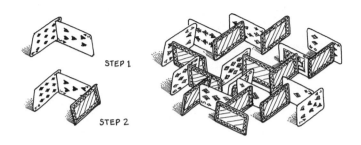

STEP 1

STEP 2

had a strong, but different, following, as did Old Maid and cribbage. To a greater or lesser degree, they still do. It simply depends on the amount of disposable time and the way it is filled (which might be innovative questions for our next census). But even in a house where big screens and video libraries dominate, odds are good that a deck of cards lingers in the closet, along with Monopoly and several boxes of jigsaw puzzles. During the next power outage, those cards may even be pressed back into service. The question is, will anyone know how to use them?

You could start with something as fundamental as building a house of cards. A builder need not know suits or numbers or face cards, and even if the deck is incomplete, it doesn't matter. In short, there are no rules. This is simply an exercise requiring steady hands, considerable patience, and oodles of time. It is easier to begin on a carpet, particularly if the house is to be a single-level, flat-roofed affair. But once a second story goes up, the parable illustrating the hazards of building a house on sand comes into play, so you might as well start on the hard surface of a table. Begin with two cards forming a T that is standing on edge, with one card leaning ever so slightly toward the other. Add a third card to either of the first two (using the same perpendicular position with a bit of a lean), but take care to make the fourth addition on the open side of the third card and try to avoid touching the first. You may find that it is easier to put a ceiling of cards on the first story before starting the second. And you could build a silo or a serpentine wall if the idle passage of time becomes a competition for the standing structure using the most cards.

More sophisticated guests may quickly expose this diversion as, well, a house of cards, so you might want to be ready with something slightly more substantive. What about a card trick? Remember the old Sim Sala Bim routine your Uncle Homer used to work? You don't have an uncle named Homer? Or you never realized it was anything less than magic? No matter, really. If you're interested it's not too hard to master. You might begin by asking for famous magic commands from the audience. "Open Sesame," "Minche Cabula," "Abracadabra," the volunteers rally. Meanwhile you have shuffled the deck several times and dealt out three piles of seven cards, each facedown. You then ask if anyone has ever used the magic words *Sim Sala Bim.* Don't worry, no one has. With practice you have worked out a story about Sim Sala Bim and how his magic skills are found in every other generation within an unrelated group of quietly powerful, completely unsuspecting believers. For all you know, someone in the room may unwittingly possess the powers of Sim Sala Bim. You have a sense that the lad who knew more than three magic commands might be just such a person. Invite that enthusiastic medium to come forward and serve as your assistant.

Start simply, asking the boy to choose one of the three piles of cards. You then pick up the chosen stack and fan it, cards facing toward the assistant and anyone else who may be interested (anyone except yourself). Ask him to select one of these seven cards and to commit it to memory—select, but don't take, just keep it in mind. As soon as you are sure this has been accomplished, fold up the fan and place the pile between the other two piles as you collect all three in your hand (try to keep the placement from being too obvious). You are holding twenty-one cards and now you deal them out as before, into three piles of seven cards each. Pick up the first pile, fan it toward the assistant, and ask if the chosen card is in that pile. If the answer is no, go to the second pile. Not there? Go to the third. It has to be in one of the three. (If it isn't, your assistant has suffered from a nervous lapse of memory and you should begin again.) Once located, but not announced—make sure your assistant understands that the location is a secret to be revealed only by Sim Sala Bim—follow the same procedure of putting the stack with the chosen card between the other two stacks. Run through this routine one more time (two identifications after the initial choosing), taking care to return the stack with the chosen card to the middle of the group. The twenty-one cards should be back in your hand, but this time, instead of dealing out three piles of seven cards, you invoke the magic of Sim Sala Bim and suggest that through its power *you* will find the card. Place one card at a time facedown on the table, spelling out the magic words S-I-M S-A-L-A B-I-M (that would be ten cards facedown). The next (eleventh) card in the pack will be the chosen one. Don't ask how! It's magic.

Success is a wondrous incentive. By the time you have mastered this trick, you may have started working on six others replete with false shuffles, marked cards, stacked decks, and a white rabbit. It is possible that someone else in the room has a little something up the sleeve or behind the ear, and so the evening goes. If it's your first time, and you wisely decide to perform the trick only two or three times (for fear the magic will wear off or logic will muscle in), it might be advisable to have a group card game in reserve. What about

Hearts or Spades, or Oh, Hell? No book of card games on the shelf? Then Hearts it is.

Or, rather, it's what Hoyle calls Omnibus Hearts, as this variation is infinitely more fun to play. You will need at least three players but no more than six, a complete deck of fifty-two cards, and some means of keeping score (the back of an envelope and a pencil will do). Fifty-two is divisible by four, which means four players will hold an even number of cards once the full deck is dealt. If you have more than four players, or fewer, take out enough low cards to make even hands. Because the player with the two of clubs leads, adjust the full count of the deck by removing the other three twos and the three of clubs. (Look at it this way: three players can play with fifty-one cards—remove one two; five can play with fifty cards—remove two twos; and six can play with forty-eight cards—remove three twos and the three of clubs.)

Before play begins, each person selects the three most heinous cards in his hand and places them facedown in a stack to be picked up by the player on the left. No fair peeking at what has been passed to you until you've pulled the worst from your hand and passed them on. What makes a card a dud? Well, for starters, each heart counts as a point against you, and high cards (the ace is highest, then king, queen, jack) win low cards, so the queen of hearts is definitely one to pass off before the game begins. Remember the two of clubs? Whoever has it wins the first lead of the game, and because the two is the lowest card, he will lose that round (or trick, as it is known in cardplaying circles), along with the opportunity to start the next round, which is why some players get rid of the two of clubs in the "pass." The queen of spades weighs in for a minus thirteen. On a more positive note, the jack of diamonds is worth ten points to the good (if you're lucky enough to end up with him at the end of the game).

So, we have a table of six players: Randy; his sister Joyce; her friend Anita; two brothers from down the hall, Bill and Timothy; and their buddy Paul. Paul is dealt the two of clubs, which he chivalrously passes to Anita, along with a couple of diamonds (they've never met before and he considers these the least offensive "bad" cards for someone who doesn't fully understand the game). Anita has handed off her rejects to Timothy and realizes in picking up the gifts from Paul (who isn't bad-looking) that she will start the game as soon as everyone else has decided what to get rid of and what to keep.

The game begins. Anita plays the two of clubs, nodding to Paul. Timothy holds the jack of clubs as well as the three and decides, using the law of averages, that for the first round everyone will probably have a club, so he can afford to play his jack, which could be the highest card played. Randy plays a four of clubs, Joyce plays the eight, Bill plays the queen, and Paul plays the ace (which, as it turns out, is the only club he holds). Paul wins that trick, since he played the highest card, and he now puts down a seven of diamonds (not too high, not too low, but because it is the first time diamonds have been played, the likelihood is that everyone will have one). Anita follows suit with her five of diamonds, Tim plays the six, Randy puts down the three, and Joyce nervously plays the ten (it's her only diamond), leaving Bill to take the trick with any diamond above the ten, if he has one. Everyone groans, Bill smiles and plays the *jack of hearts* (since he never did have any diamonds he can play whatever card he likes). Joyce takes the trick and with it her first negative point (thanks to the jack of hearts). She then leads with the three of spades, essentially handing the game to someone else in hopes of avoiding any more tricks with those nasty hearts.

It's an understandable move. Nobody likes to win hearts. Well, almost nobody. The exception may arise if you find yourself with a hand that is loaded with face cards from each suit and also a string of high cards in one particular suit, which means you could take a majority (maybe even all) of the tricks. Do it. At the end of the game, if you have won each and every heart, plus the queen of spades and the jack of diamonds, you will be awarded twenty-six points for "shooting the moon." You must be terribly clever to figure out from what is passed and what you hold where the cards are and how you will get them, all the while feigning dismay when the first hearts begin to appear in the tricks you are winning. But as you are busily rounding up those hearts, remember, even the best of friends will snag a heart or two to avert a coup.

The hour is late, and a few of the players are beginning to yawn and stretch and think about tomorrow. Joyce is about to realize a sibling's fantasy by besting her brother Randy. Bill and Timothy are recalling one hilarious childhood prank with predictable twists: Bill says it was Tim's idea (and he's calling home in the morning to prove it), but Tim actually remembers only hearing about it (he's sure he was at a friend's house playing cards at the time). Meanwhile, Paul is trying to figure out how to see Anita again in the same casual, uncommitted setting, and he is toying with extending an invitation to continue the game next Saturday at his apartment. And to think it all started with a little deck of cards.

Playing Charades

It's well after the dinner hour, the kitchen counters are clear, the dishes have been washed, dried, and put away. The guests managed to exhaust every possible form of small talk during your predinner preparations, and just the slightest mention of politics produced enough smoke to clear the dining room after dessert. But before you begin the all-American search for the remote, consider the alternatives. Someone with a particularly good voice could read from the collected works of Robert W. Service or, if you happen to have multiple copies of anything, several guests could form a readers' theater troupe. Maybe someone in the crowd (the one who usually brings a guitar) would like to sing. Then again, perhaps none of the guests has a song in his heart, because it's a farewell dinner held on the eve of a cross-country move. And it follows that every volume of poetry has been boxed and carried to the van. But you can always play charades, a remarkable game that requires nothing more than a degree of cultural literacy, something to write with, something to write on, a lack of inhibition, and a clock.

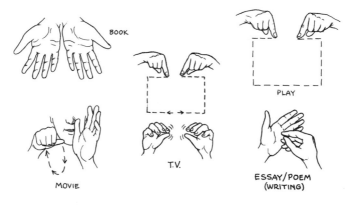

Charades is a challenge to communicate without words. It is unofficially played when two people who do not speak the same language must exchange critical information. Where is the nearest toilet? Did the bus already leave? What's a great-looking person like you doing in a place like this? But instead of genuine, urgent questions, *official* charades is concerned with titles—titles of books, songs, plays, poems, essays, short stories, movies, television programs, and quotations. (True, quotations aren't titles, but they can be terrifically challenging to act out.)

Each of these categories has a signal that should be demonstrated to the entire group before the game begins. If the title is a movie, make a camera: hold your left hand flat, thumb to nose; making a fist with your right hand, move it in a circular manner against the palm of the left hand as if

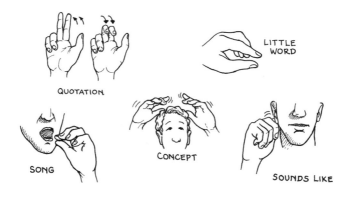

QUOTATION

LITTLE WORD

SONG

CONCEPT

SOUNDS LIKE

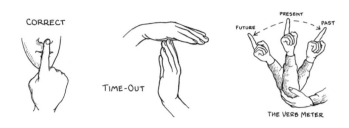

CORRECT

TIME-OUT

PRESENT

FUTURE — — → PAST

THE VERB METER

you were drawing repeated circles. If it's a play, draw the outline of a rectangle, signifying a stage. If it's a book, put your hands together, palms up, the edges of your pinkies touching. If it's a song, pull an imaginary sound from your open mouth. If it's a poem, essay, or short story, write on your palm. For a television show, draw the outline of a rectangle and then adjust the knobs at the bottom of the "screen." And if you'll be doing a quotation, use your index and middle fingers to form quotation marks, bending them up and down.

Charades is played with two teams. Try to choose teams that will be relatively even. Competitive couples should be split up, children should be fairly distributed, aspiring actors should not outnumber computer science majors. You get the drift. The teams are sequestered in separate rooms to come up with titles—at least one for every player on the other team. The titles are written down on individual pieces of paper (it may be helpful to include the category as well);

they are then folded and gathered together for an opposing team member to choose from when his turn comes. No fair giving a player a certain title just because you're dying to see her struggle with *The Unbearable Lightness of Being.* And keep in mind that while the esoteric is desirable, if no one on the opposing team has ever heard of that privately printed collection of Japanese haiku, and they can't figure it out, the time the team spent guessing is not included in the final tally. In other words, you don't get rewarded for completely stumping them and they don't lose anything either.

While you are writing down all your tricky titles and quotations, try to come up with a plan ("How would we act this out?") for each one suggested by your team. The exercise will help you twice: first by disqualifying any selections that are really too easy and again by giving your team some rehearsal should the same title or quotation be presented by your opponents.

As soon as both teams are ready, a volunteer (probably someone who has been playing charades for years) agrees to go first and picks a slip of paper from the opposing team. The player is then given a moment to come up with a plan before facing his own team. He may need to confer with a member of the opposing team if the clue on the paper is illegible or possibly incorrect (you think the King James version reads, "In the beginning was the Word," and the paper you have selected reads, "From the beginning was the Word"). Once the player declares he is ready, however, he is no longer allowed to talk, whinny, or bray.

The team not guessing keeps track of the time. Three to five minutes is considered an acceptable amount of time to guess a title. Depending upon the options presented by the title, this may seem too short; on the other hand, semiprofessionals have been known to send notes of apology for exceeding a twenty-five-second personal best (since the team that uses the least time wins, every second counts). The opposing team should try to be quiet (mothers must resist the urge to blurt answers to their children's befuddled teammates, siblings should refrain from encouraging miscommunication with distracting guffaws and loud whispering).

There are certain signals to keep in mind as you are working on your plan of attack. Correct answers are noted by putting your index finger to the tip of your nose (as in "on the nose"). You should also show your teammates how many words are in the title (decide what the word limit will be before anyone begins coming up with titles). And consider whether it is possible to act out the general idea. The signal for "concept" is to move your hands three inches above your head as if you were shampooing. This means that you are about to act out the general idea behind the title instead of taking a more literal approach (you *become* the wolf who blows down the pigs' house). The concept approach may or may not prove to be productive; you should have a plan B that involves clues for at least three key words.

And that's not all. You can break a long word into syllables by showing your teammates a series of numbers. "There are seven words" is indicated by holding up seven fingers; then hold up three fingers and it means "And this is the third word." Next, "It has five syllables" is indicated by holding up five fingers, and "This is the fourth syllable" by immediately holding up four fingers. It is critical that everyone is working on the right syllable of the right word, so find someone on your team who seems to be keeping up with you and establish eye contact, pointing to your nose for every correct answer.

By the way, holding your index finger parallel to your extended thumb (the standard sign for "little") indicates a word of two or three letters. Your team should be ready with a steady stream of guesses: "the, an, but, is, at, in, on, for."

Often a word or syllable is easier to convey through rhyming. *Going My Way*, for instance, might be more quickly won if it were presented as *Sewing Bye Pay*. Just give a tug on your earlobe for "rhymes with," and be sure to look directly at the teammate who comes up with the right word (point to your nose). There is nothing more time-consuming or confusing than a team of rhyming fools who have quite lost sight of which syllable or words they are working on and have become remarkably self-absorbed in a recitation of the alphabet. They mean well, but for you they have become dysfunctional. Stop the game with a referee's capital **T** time-out signal, quickly reestablish what was in place before the babbling began (it's a movie; first word, little word; second word, five syllables; second syllable, sounds like . . .), and continue on with a new approach.

There are a few other helpful signals, such as the verb meter. Hold your right elbow in the palm of your left hand to resemble Ted Mack's applause meter: future tense (to the far right), present (center), and past (to the left). Gerunds, past participles, anything that makes a word longer, is signaled by a taffy-pulling motion.

No sound is allowed, and neither are props. Rather than bringing a boot in from the mudroom, you must illustrate it by indicating its shape, where it is worn, or how it is taken off. Pointing to someone whose name appears in the title or rhymes with one of the words also falls under the no props rule. When you are deciding on a limit to the number of words in titles, you should also mention that the game will be played in English, unless, of course, you are in an international group, and then you may spend some time developing signals for whatever language you might be using.

Which brings us to the sensitive subject of the diverging

road. When it comes to acting out titles, one path leads along a high and difficult moral ledge, the other slips down to more fertile ground. The low road will definitely make a lasting impression, and it is often the quicker way home. Competitive impulses aside, there is always the matter of Taste. Consider your audience, your host, your reputation . . . the choice is yours. It has nothing to do with charades. Above all, think of this section as if it were the inside of the top of a Scrabble box. Rules are for reference. Beginners only need to know some basic signals and restriction on making sounds. Assurances are well founded; stage fright will subside. By the end of the last round, ten to one the avid will be surpassed by the converted.

More Family Fun

OUTDOOR ENTERTAINMENTS

❖

Californians will tell you, not all parties happen indoors. Picnics at the beach, hikes in the mountains, an afternoon game of croquet, there's just all sorts of fun waiting out there in the open. Along with this wide expanse comes welcome freedom to move, shout, to cavort without crashing into walls or waking the baby. The sky's the limit! Run, skip, jump till you drop. Yodel at will (or as you will). There's nothing like the great outdoors to evoke exuberance. That is, unless you are completely uncomfortable in new or unfamiliar surroundings. Consider the happy world of a two-year-old who busily plays with brightly colored toys in a climate-controlled playroom day in and day out. She can show you where the potty is *and* how to use it. Now take the same child, or an older sibling, or any adult who counts rushing from the car to the train-station platform as an outdoor activity, and let her loose in the open countryside. The lack of toilet facilities is noticed right away, followed by a longing for Legos, a favorite television show, a book, a comfortable place to sit. Well, never mind. There are more toys and shows and stories to be found in the fields than anyone ever found in the house. You just have to know where to look. (HINT: Start by thinking, what are you not allowed to do inside? Ah, freedom.)

Doing a Headstand and a Cartwheel

Not all dinner tables are graced with linen napkins and crystal goblets. Some rely on paper plates and plastic forks. They're called barbecues. Others call for nesting aluminum ware. They're called camp-outs. As the atmosphere shifts from stuffy to casual, so does the dress code. Shirtsleeves and shorts stand in for jackets and long skirts. And it isn't simply a change in wardrobe. Your talent need no longer be confined to the dining room. Your theater is now of greater proportion. It's all of the outdoors, or at least as much of it as you might wish to use. So why not try something you've always wanted to do but weren't sure you could?

Let's start with a headstand for confidence-building. Resist the notion that gymnastics are for the young. Age is a question raised only by the impudent. Recall Father William. In fact, you might consider reciting the poem as you upend yourself, especially if your hair is turning white. For reference, then:

"You are old, Father William," the young man said,
"And your hair has become very white;
And yet you incessantly stand on your head—
Do you think, at your age, it is right?"

"In my youth," Father William replied to his son
"I feared it might injure the brain;
But now that I'm perfectly sure I have none,
Why, I do it again and again."

While you're running the verse through your head, once for words only and twice for accent and tone, look for level ground. Truth to tell, you might consider practicing this inside (in which case you should look for the thickest carpet), facing a wall to prevent a nasty fall. Assume a squatting position, that is, with your knees bent and your arms between your legs. Hands, shoulder-distance apart, are resting on the floor. Remember playing leap frog? It should look like you're about to play it again. Slowly roll your head down to a point on the floor slightly in front of your hands. This position is the "tripod," defined by its three points. We learned about it in geometry and wondered when it would become useful information. Now it has.

As your head goes down, your knees should roll onto your upper arms just above the elbows (see the illustration). How's the balance? Feeling steady? Good. Now for the incredible finale. With your legs still tucked in, lift your hips so that they are directly over your head. Imagine a drum roll. Take it slowly. This trick is much more impressive when it unfolds and holds on the first try. Gradually stretch your legs straight up and point your toes. Think of Nadia Comaneci. While you are waiting for applause, look to see that no one is standing close enough to suffer the ill effects of a rapid descent.

Ready to return your face to a more natural color? Reverse the procedure: tuck your head (chin to chest); bend your legs and bring your knees down to rest on your elbows; let your feet touch the floor; you have landed. When you are no longer dependent on the security of a wall and you wish to add additional flair, turn the headstand into phase one of a somersault. Remember to tuck your head and put enough conviction (or force) into the roll to bring you to your feet, not your back. (Also remember that discretion is the better part of valor.)

If Lewis Carroll can inspire you to perform a headstand,

Headstand

Leonardo da Vinci may help you envision a cartwheel. His famous drawing of a human form in a circle offers conclusive proof of human cartwheel capability. What? Is there a murmur of doubt rippling through the room? Go ahead, stand up. Even better, stand up in front of a mirror. Spread your legs and stretch out your arms, think of yourself as a human **X**. According to Leonardo, the position fits neatly inside a circle, touching at four points. Your limbs are like four spokes of a wheel.

Keeping that anatomical potential in mind, stand with your toes pointing straight ahead. The path of a cartwheel follows at a right angle to your toes, which is the first instance of believing. You know the path is clear, you have looked at

Cartwheel

it to see that it is relatively level and free of sticks and stones. But while you are actually doing the cartwheel, you will be looking straight ahead—not in the direction you are going, but in the direction you are facing. It is in some sense a blind act of faith.

Does your mind still hold a picture of the pose? Good, because now it is time to assume it. Knees locked, legs straight, feet about two feet apart (so that they are directly below your shoulders), arms raised with elbows locked and hands spread to distribute weight and help with balance. There is one moment when this position changes. In order to get the wheel rolling, you will need to gather some momentum by lifting your right leg, bending the knee, rocking to the left ever so slightly, and then throwing your weight to the right while thrusting your extended left leg skyward. CAUTION: This point is often the beginning of a flawed effort. Here you may lose a straight back by bending to the left from the waist, which means that your right hand is that much farther from making contact with the ground. Remember, you are breaking with the limbs-as-spokes position only momentarily, to gain momentum. As soon as it is achieved, legs, arms, and back should be straight and properly spaced. It is precisely at this moment that flashes of self-doubt, of regret, of fear, of utter humiliation will pass through your mind like so many episodes of your life. Take heart.

You are not anywhere near a body of water, you are no farther from the ground whether you are resting on your feet or your hands, and the only thing that will make you topple over onto your backside will be a loss of concentration.

It may be helpful to have a rhythm worked out, right foot being "one," right hand being "two," left hand "three," and left foot "four," followed by the right foot "one" (should you be performing in multiple revolutions) or "Brava" (if you were planning to do only one). A smooth, even rhythm uttered while holding a picture of the correct position in your mind may be enough to crowd out distracting fears and put doubts on hold. It's sort of the Lamaze approach to gymnastics. Think about the steps, think about the form, count while panting if it helps, just don't let the thought of your own upper-body weakness enter the formula. When you are upside down, your head should tilt back just enough to focus on a point exactly between, and just in front of, your hands. If your motion gets stuck in this handstand position, you may have to give a slight bend-thrust-kick with your left leg to continue. Remember to keep every contact—hands, eyes, feet—on the same straight path.

NOTE: This is not a slow-motion event. Speed is a significant element of a successful cartwheel. Think of a hoop or a coin. The faster it rolls along its rim, the longer it stays upright. As it slows, it wobbles and eventually falls to one side. Full speed ahead now. No more interruptions. Envision, count, breathe, you are standing, tilting to the left, hurling to your right, right hand touches the ground, now the left (you're looking directly at the center point), right hand leaves the ground as left foot descends, and back up on your feet. Congratulations! You made it, full circle.

Dancing a Jig

The perfect party piece requires more than just the willingness and ability to perform. Yes, the cartwheel demands physical prowess and the magic trick requires confounding dexterity. But well before you begin the performance you face the challenge of stage-setting. This is the time to lead your audience by the hand, making every connection between whatever has brought you together and the way you have chosen to mark the event. Setting the stage is rather like the fashion designer's secret: *accessorize.* The simple linen shift can be dressed up or down to fit almost any occasion. And your unrivaled mastery of just one entertaining skill can carry you for a long time. Consider, for example, the jig. You've spent hours hopping about in front of a full-length mirror humming "The Nutting Girl" in ¾ time, you've committed the steps to memory, and you are ready to dance whenever it seems appropriate. So take the occasion at hand and milk it for all it's worth. Is it the high-carbohydrate pasta feed before the marathon? Then your audience is presumably fit and eager to learn new forms of aerobic expression. Is it in honor of Uncle Robb, who has taken a week between shows to visit his new niece? You are suddenly reminded of William Kempe, Mr. Shakespeare's favorite comic lead, who once jigged all the way from London to Norwich . . . it was Kempe's Nine-Day Wonder. Are you celebrating the summer solstice, election day, or passing through Mahoosuc Notch? Learning to dance a jig takes practice; fitting it to an occasion takes imagination. Stretching is encouraged in either case.

Solo dances are found in most cultures, performed as often by the esteemed leader as by the fool. The steps can involve frantic whirling or genteel bowing, alternating pointed toes or leg thrusts from a squatting position, and each step has a name and a tradition and a band of scholars who may themselves be tireless dancers. So as not to step on any toes . . . notations for the jig you are about to learn are as follows. It is a derivation of a Morris jig of the Bampton tradition danced in jig (%) or reel (¼) time, which also means that the steps could be found in any one of eight jigs from that region of England. By tradition, they were danced as part of a spring ritual. The easiest way to establish a jig time, and indeed to perform the dance, is to bring along a fiddler who has been playing jigs since he was a wee lad. If that is not an option, ask if there is anyone present who knows the tune to "Greensleeves" (also known at Christmastime as "What Child Is This?"). With any luck, two or three murmurs will swell into a chorus, which you may encourage by offering an exchange, your dancing for their humming. But if no one even nods, you may decide to sing while you dance (which is, after all, what you've been doing every time you practice the jig), or you may have chosen the wrong party piece, or both. One thing is certain: he who does not know the tune is not master of the jig. And in the absence of a master, the fool is king.

Tempting as it may be, let's not allow a rise in confidence to be based solely on the ignorance of others. There are some basic idiosyncrasies that mark a Morris dance. Dancers stand with shoulders back and heads erect. The steps are taken as if by a single-jointed marionette, with alternate legs swinging, front to back, from the hip with only the slightest bending of the knee (and no pointing of the toes). Don't be discouraged. Stand in front of a mirror and start whistling the tune. Shift your weight from the ball of your left foot to that of your right following the rhythm of the tune (stepping on the accented beat). As soon as you are comfortable with stepping in place, try stepping *out*. Swing your right foot out in front on the heavy beat (not too far or you'll fall over) and land on the ball of that foot on the next, weaker beat (it's just like hopping, for heaven's sake, only in a more stylized and initially self-conscious manner). Imagine that your calves are adorned with wide bands of bells (standard Morris garb). As you become more steady in this basic step, moving backward and forward, try shaking the swinging leg and giving a bit more spring to the takeoff and landing. Ring those bells, wake up the earth, and maybe even one or two of your fellow guests who look like they'd rather be dancing than humming.

But wait, the jig is more than repeating a single motion forward for four counts and back for another four. Embellishment is expected in this business. Let's try a caper. It's nothing more than a grand Morris step—higher, fuller, bigger. To make the point, your hands, which traditionally rest on the hips throughout the jig, may be flung, first up and then out. A true caper takes up two full beats (as you may have suspected, a half caper takes only one). And if you happen to have access to white napkins or handkerchiefs, hold them in your hands to add to the flourish of the caper.

Then there is a "side step," a crossing of one foot in front of the other, which can be done in place or on the move. For the time being, forget about hopping and think about rocking. Cross your right foot in front of your left foot, twisting at the waist so that your right shoulder is above the right foot, which now supports you. Rock back onto the left foot and then forward onto the right. That's it, back and forth. In order to change sides, you will have to do a little hop on the eighth beat. It goes like this: cross right, rock back to left, cross right, rock back to left, cross right, rock back to left, cross right, hop right, then SWITCH, cross left, rock back to right, cross left, back right, cross left, back right, cross left, hop left, SWITCH, cross right . . . Get it? Try it again. Don't forget those shoulders. Head up? Smiling? Singing? And how are those thighs holding up?

Side Step

A Bampton jig includes a sequence of side steps, capers, and standard steps. It is meant to be a lively entertainment, meaning "Greensleeves" needs to be pepped up a bit. Or choose a different tune. Once you've settled on the score, work out the math and match the beats to the steps. For instance, the sequence of side steps outlined above would take eight strong beats, or the first two measures of "Greensleeves," whereas two Morris steps and a caper would require only four strong beats. Write down the sequence of your choosing. Some like to start slowly and end with a flourish, others begin and end with a caper, side stepping every which way throughout the middle. At this point it's up to you. Trouble remembering the progression? Tie the steps to the lyrics or use them as alternate lyrics (think of those recordings of Glenn Gould playing the piano while singing to himself).

Practice can wear you out. Fatigue may slowly dissolve earlier dreams of a public performance. But your heart (which is strengthening with every rehearsal) should not be given immediate heed. By the time this jig of yours is mastered, you will be in much better shape than you are now—and remember, jigs by definition are brief. Dancing through a tune twice will take only a minute or two. Only a minute or two did you say? That's right, unless of course you decide over the period of a month of daily rehearsals that you're really quite given to this sort of thing (in which case the first jig you labored through now pales in comparison to the intricacies of your latest number and you're starting to think about retracing Kempe's route to Norwich). Remember, no strain, no gain.

A caution: Your jig will not be an official Morris jig, as any fellow in a green hat with colorful ribbon streamers will tell you. Don't apologize, just ask to see *his* favorite jig. Trade techniques, share lamb's wool. And look at it this way, the only one who isn't dancing correctly is the one who is still sitting.

Making a Daisy Chain

A few white clouds hang in the west . . . not to threaten but to catch the afterglow of the sunset. A loose game of baseball is beginning to need an umpire. Someone's kite is luffing. There is an extra blanket if anyone wants to nap, and the crossword puzzle isn't finished. Everyone is enjoying a Sunday-afternoon picnic. Well, almost everyone. You hear a small voice saying, "I have nothing to do," followed by, "Me either." Too little to catch with a glove, too big to fit in a Gerry pack, two tykes whose tummies are full and bubble-juice bottles are empty wander into the peace zone.

"Did you see Uncle John's kite?"

"Yep, but he said we couldn't hold the string."

"Can you find the tennis ball to throw for Spot?"

"Spot's sleeping. There's nothing to do."

Grandpa rolls onto his side and does what he can to muffle the voices with his cap.

"You could make daisy chains."

"I don't know how to."

"I could show you how to make them, but first we need to find some daisies. I think there are some down by the stream." You bid a silent farewell to the crossword puzzle and the angels place another star in your crown.

There are some basic rules to consider in making daisy chains. The first is to use only prolific, wild, unendangered flowers growing in the public domain. Daisies are the best because of their size and because of a four-year-old's fixation with labels, but many other field flowers (Indian paintbrush, red clover, even the smaller white clover and dandelions found in most playing fields and pastures) will work just as well. The key to a successful chain is not the size or color of the blossom but the shape and texture of the stem. It needs to be flexible and at the same time have enough fiber to withstand a slight incision. In other words, it can't be woody or stiff and it can't be delicate or thin (lilacs and forget-me-nots won't do).

Pick a handful of flowers with stems three or more inches in length. The longer the stem, the greater the margin for error. About half an inch from the end of the stem, make a slit using your thumbnail, or a knife if your thumbnail is too short. Holding the stem in both hands just above and just below the cut, push your fingers together and open the hole, taking care to keep it from tearing at the bottom. How big should the hole be? As big as the solid center of the flower. Pass the blossom through the hole (fold the daisy petals into the center so they won't tear off) and then pull at either end of the hole so that it closes just behind the flower. The stem, which was once a straight line from ground to blossom, is now a ring. In fact, it's the first link of your first chain.

This production is rarely smooth. Stems split and links

weaken or break. Gatherers may deliver fistfuls of blossoms with little or no stem at all. Small motor skills are required along with infinite patience. Presumably time is what you have to spare, and with practice you will eventually have a charming necklace. Happily, evidence of something worth waiting for appears almost immediately as you link the first circle to the second and the second to the third. But your audience may grow tired of watching, and all your good intentions of keeping them entertained may become like so many bricks paving that infamous road.

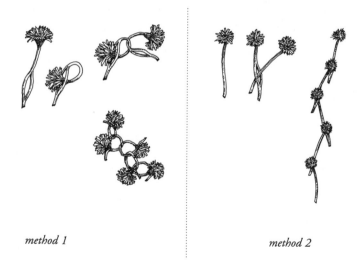

method 1   *method 2*

There is another method, one not as finished because the stems are left to stick out willy-nilly and the effect is wispy in an unruly sort of way. But it is definitely easier for the novice and it takes much less time, so consider using this technique if: (1) cordons or bridal trains are the aim; (2) the labor force is significantly underage; or (3) the stems are very short. Rather than pushing the head of the flower through the slit at the base of the stem, you simply pass the stem of a second flower through the slit of the first until the head rests against the stem (in this method, make the slit about an inch below the blossom). Make a slit in the second flower's stem (again, about an inch below the blossom) and pass a third flower through it. And so on, until you have achieved the desired length. There remains the problem of a clasp (unless you've decided to wear the garland draped several times around your neck with the ends dangling, as one imagines poor Ophelia must have done). Tying the ends in a loose bow or making a link at both ends (using the first method) should solve the problem.

Eventually the process becomes more or less tiresome and questions of usefulness make their way into the conversation. What good are these daisy chains? What's to be done with them? Discussions of vision and purpose, mission and future occur outside the boardroom as often as they do inside. And so you set about helping them to define the market. The family has been waiting for an announcement from Mia and Fergus for at least six years; maybe the presentation of two leis would do the trick. Someone special has planned, prepared, and packed this wonderful picnic—service worthy of a most beautiful crown. Maybe everyone should have a boa—and a ring and a belt, too. There must be one hundred uses for daisy chains. Just wait until Saint-Laurent catches these coming down the runway.

Predicting the Weather

The alarm goes off. It's 6:25 A.M., just in time for the weather report. "A cold front moving down from Canada should bring some pretty heavy rain into our region by the middle of the day." You make a mental note to take an umbrella. Waiting for your coffee, you double-check WPOR's forecast against the Weather Channel's map. Sure enough, there is that cloud-with-rain symbol hanging right over the city's head. You consider carrying your shoes and wearing boots. What does the morning paper predict? You open the door to find that the paper is wet despite its plastic sleeve. "What's this middle-of-the-day stuff?" you say, putting your hand out the door for verification. "It's pouring right now!"

With any luck, when you were young you had the freedom to spend considerable time lying on your back watching the clouds change from dragons to castles, from spinnakers to swans. You didn't own a watch . . . you were told to be home before dark. When you were older and time was less likely to be squandered in sky-gazing (more probably divided between idle chat and binge exam-cramming), clouds were most immediately significant as a quick and dirty means of identification: a Fragonard or a Watteau? The art history exam was precisely at 2:00—whatever the weather. Somewhere along the way, you managed to gain a practical awareness—a cause-and-effect sort of thing—clouds bring wet weather.

Well, not all clouds. As it turns out, some clouds only announce the arrival of a storm in the next day or so. Others catch a ride on a friendly airstream and float by with an ethereal, whispered "Have a nice tomorrow." In one short lesson (or, if you were in the Scouts, a review), you can decrease your dependency on the instrument-bound, windowless, early-morning forecasters and develop a built-in excuse for watching the clouds go by at your leisure. With practice, you could become the trusted weather oracle for your office. Given the universal human fascination with the weather, you will not only be a regular guest at picnics (your acceptance means more than your good company), you will also be capable of offering the longest-running entertainment . . . the show is from dawn to dusk.

This lesson could be entitled Weather 101: forecasting in

its most basic form. It is presented for the would-be amateur as a first step (and for the much-scorned meteorologists as a last laugh). It begins with the obvious components—wind, temperature, and water—the three factors to bear in mind. Wind from a given direction changes the land temperature, causing water on the ground to rise up and form clouds in the sky. And when those clouds are weighted down with too much water, they open up and sprinkle, dribble, or pour the water back down to the ground. The sequence usually looks something like this: blue sky, high white clouds, wind, gray sky, low dark clouds, precipitation, wind, dispersing clouds, blue sky. The progression may take two hours or it may take ten days, but it usually follows the same pattern. This isn't anything you don't know. Just like a tired joke or a rusty sleight of hand, it is no surprise to your audience either. Relax. You won't open with this material. But background information is important (just ask your grandmother, the one who mercilessly vetted every single one of your mother's suitors). It builds credibility into your act.

Now it's time to take a look at the sky. How high do you think those wispy white clouds are? They used to be called mares' tails because of the way they curl up at the end. Sometimes they look more like a spider's web or a hen's feathers—thin strands that may or may not form a pattern and don't look like much of a threat. Well, as it turns out, they are as high as clouds go, which means they are made up of ice particles. And if the wind is coming out of the west and heading north, they are harmless. But if the wind is blowing out of the east or northeast and heading south, they are trying to tell you that tomorrow's picnic is going to be held indoors.

Sounds like the next step is to figure out which way the wind is blowing. The assumption is that because the six of you have been picnicking at this spot for as long as you can remember, no one brought a compass. Fact A: the sun rises in the east and sets in the west. Fact B: in the middle of the day, fact A is not particularly helpful. You ask the group, "Where is true south?" You can see how this question alone could be yanked from its context and generate an afternoon's worth of opinion and debate . . . do what you can to stay the course by showing them a crude but relatively accurate way to determine the answer you were looking for. You will need a plumb line and a level, which, like the compass, nobody thought to bring along. In their place, you could borrow five or six yards from the end of Janie's kite string—she's such a willing child—and tie a rock or a spoon or whatever you can find to give some weight to one end (having secured the other end to the picnic hamper). Toss the weight of choice (the string will follow) over a gracefully extended tree limb (you are picnicking in the shade of a tree, are you not?).

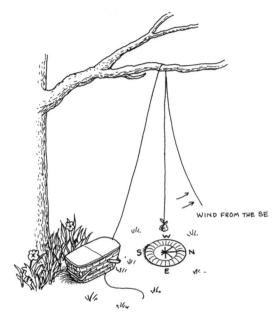

WIND FROM THE SE

That's the plumb line. Next, do what you can to make the surface below the dangling string level-ish. It won't be perfect. But if it's perceptibly sloping and you are in the company of perfectionists, consider building a subfloor by using whatever flotsam and jetsam is lying about to shore up a proper plate. Is it level? The marble in your pocket (or a hard-boiled egg) will provide the answer. If it rolls off the plate, the answer is no, so do what you can to even it up. All set? Congratulations, you have before you a makeshift sundial. (The question is, do you still have an audience? If the answer is yes, by all means proceed.)

At "absolute" noon (not a time given on your wristwatch —it varies considerably from that noon depending on the time of year and where you are standing on the globe), the plumb line's shadow will be the shortest. That shadow will also point toward true south (or, depending on which way you face, toward true north). Ask for volunteers who would be willing to measure the shadows during the course of the day (Janie and her younger brother Ross raise their hands). They should start marking at 11:00 A.M. (according to your watch), give or take a quarter hour. Little sticks staked in the ground to mark the shadow's position and length, or lines drawn on the plate at roughly fifteen-minute intervals, will chart the sun's course from east to west. As soon as you can determine the north-south line, you can be sure of the east-west line and get on with the question at hand. Remember? It was "Which way is the wind blowing?"

Now, take the weight off the string and turn your plumb line into a weather vane. You've already determined the points of the compass on the ground below the string, so, as the string moves with the wind, take a look at its shadow. If it is angling from east to south, your silky strands of high-flying clouds are telling you about some rain that will arrive in about twenty-four hours. If the shadow lines up in a west-to-north direction, you can start planning for another day of sunshine.

What if the clouds aren't wispy? What if they are big cotton-ball clumps? If those clumps are somewhat uniform, that is, if they look like the top of a single-scoop ice-cream cone, and the wind is negligible, they are fair-weather clouds —known in scientific terms as cumulus humilis—bet you can't say that without smiling. But if they begin to look like triple-scoop cones or drip castles, and instead of being bright white their outlines turn a menacing gray, and the wind is picking up out of the northeast and heading south, they are known as cumulus fractus. And if they are moving in front of a blanket of gray, they are cumulus congestus— the sky's version of a serious head cold. In either case, it is probably time to think about how long it took you to hike to the picnic site. By the way, if anyone can identify an anvil

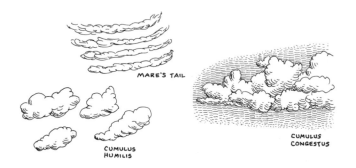

MARE'S TAIL

CUMULUS HUMILIS

CUMULUS CONGESTUS

shape among those darkening clouds, everyone should be encouraged to pick up the pace on the way home.

Low clouds that blanket the sky and look like a washboard or a dirt road in August can make for a magnificent sunset. And if the wind is out of the northeast blowing south? You guessed it. Rain is likely within the next twelve to twenty-four hours. Speaking of sunsets, the sky's colors are another indication of approaching weather. Most everyone knows the old saw "Red sky at morning, sailors take warning; red sky at night, sailor's delight." There are at least two provisos, though. It's a *cloudless* night sky reflecting the color of a sinking, fiery red ball that makes for a sure sign of clear weather in the morning. And it's a blanket of clouds turned red (not orange or pink or lavender or whatever falls in between, but an even red) that's the warning—at sunrise *or* sunset. A multicolored sunset, with purples and yellows playing around the edges of those rose-hued puffs, generally means fair weather, at least for the next day. In contrast, a colorless sunset (when the sun turns a blue sky bright white as it sinks behind dark gray clouds) means rain is on the way.

Jim confesses he missed last night's sunset. Gladys was inside all of yesterday and didn't take any notice of the sky. More's the pity, agreed, but do what you can to refrain from sighing. Assume that there are those who notice the weather only when they are forced out into it, and offer them a verse or two:

> Evening fogs will not burn soon
> Morning fog will burn 'fore noon
> Fog that starts before the night
> Will last beyond the morning light.

Or one that has buoyed the weepy bride and her anxious mother:

> Rain before seven
> will end by eleven.

Tell them about the gossamer linens (commonly thought to be spiders' webs stretched out on the morning lawn). No self-respecting fairy would put the laundry out on a rainy day! Now really. See for yourself, the skies will be blue by noon. And should there be any lingering doubts, suggest logging predictions and rating them. Nothing like pitting yourself against the professionals, not to mention the gods.

More Fun Out-of-Doors

WEEKEND ENTERTAINMENTS

❖

"Andy and I are thinking of renting a big old beach house with a bunch of people next July . . . the usual suspects . . . want to come?" The idea sounded good in December. Even after loading up for the long, hot, sticky drive and unloading in a cloud of mosquitoes, it still sounds good. No television, no phone, no papers, that was the vision. No insulated walls, no sound system, no microwave, that's the reality. But this vacation away from the familiar creature comforts is a matter of choice. It's also a considerable amount of time without the familiar patterns of comings and goings that lend structure to life. No deadlines to gobble up entire days, no reports to devour nights, no school assemblies or soccer practices or cleaners-before-closing to race to. Suddenly time is unfettered. At first everyone feels slightly unglued. Watches are synchronized, plans to keep current with the national news are made, activities are planned (where, when, and how long). There is a scramble to regain control. If the vacation is of sufficient length, all this scurrying dies down like so much steam in a kettle pulled from the fire. Then there is an almost dreamlike quality to the hours that pass unaccounted.

Though jolted from the complacency of your everyday

rut, you (the perfect guest) are not dazed, but invigorated. Knowing that a lull often precedes a storm, you seize the opportunity provided by this peaceful calm to organize projects. Who wants to make kites? Who knows how to juggle? Who can find the Big Dipper? With nothing but time on their hands, those who might become bored are now obsessed with practicing. Can't you just hear it? Twenty years from now someone will marvel at the confidence with which she juggles the Waterford. "Well, I first got interested when my parents took the world's longest and rainiest vacation in a big old beach house on an island off the coast of Maine. A friend of theirs brought along a bag of marshmallows . . ." Kudos from afar.

Making a Glider and a Kite

The Sunday-afternoon doldrums seep through the house. Brunch was great, the paper was good for a clipping or two, home base has been reached and reassured (Granny had a decent round of golf, Pop is planning to watch some tennis). Sandy called to see what was cookin' in the neighborhood (their TV has been on the blink since anyone can remember and their kids need to find a new channel for excess energy). They blow in an hour later and now the household numbers nine. Washing up in the kitchen leads to a caucus. The sun is shining, there's a breeze coming out of the west, and a course of action is chosen accordingly. Sandy will show any interested kids how to make very good, never-fail gliders, while Brooks will try to rustle up some kite string and tape—which ultimately means a trip to the store. "While you're there, how about a box of reinforcing rings . . . you know, they look like small paper lifesavers, yeah, we used to use them back in the days of three-ring notebooks." Pat has to leave to make her rounds and she offers to drop Brooks at the store on her way to the hospital; she'll meet up with everyone later in the park. Alex heads upstairs to get a stack of computer paper (used, but not for anything that should be shredded) and a good set of felt-tip markers for kite decoration. Where are the scissors?

A glider needs to have a significant wingspan and just the right ballast. The modern Styrofoam version of yesterday's balsa fighters comes with a plastic nose clip to assure a long, steady flight (never mind an endless lifetime). With careful folding, borrowing a subtle origami-ish style, you can make one every bit as good as any store-bought model without bulking the lines of the design. Using a plain old ordinary piece of paper, measuring the standard 8½" × 11", make a lengthwise fold. It is important to keep every side even from the beginning. Do the edges match up? Great. Unfold the paper so it assumes its original shape. Using the center crease as a guide, bring in the top corners (1 and 2 in the illustration) to meet it and down to form two triangles. Bring down the top, center point (3), making a crease along the bottom of the two triangles. This is where the scissors come into play. Fold the plane along the original lengthwise crease and clip two squares (roughly an inch across) from the outside edges. Open the paper along the center crease so the cut-out squares are on the right and left sides. Bring the new top corners (4 and 5 in the illustration) to the center crease and down to form two triangles (with missing squares), which should cover all but the tip of the first triangle folds. Pull up

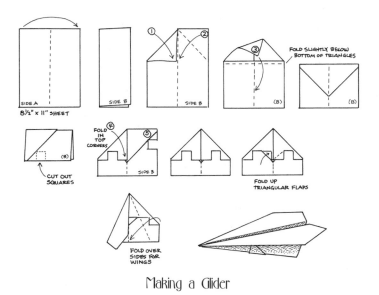

Making a Glider

the small flaps (4 and 5), fold them along the line made by the cut-out squares, and bring the outside edges of the wings toward the center. Reach in and take hold of the middle cluster of folds (they are the body of the plane), folding the wings back along the original vertical fold; tighten the creases; put your arm back; alert bystanders; elevate the nose; and throw. Bingo! You did it.

Kites don't offer the same degree of instant gratification. The flip side is, the experience lasts much longer. That's part of their magic. You can begin by decorating a piece of paper (8½" × 11" is perfect for a kite that needs only a little wind). On the back side of the paper, draw an X using the four corners as guides. From the top of the kite, follow one inch from the corners along the diagonal lines and make a hole (if you have reinforcers, this is where they can be used—one on each side; if you don't strengthen the edges with a little bit of tape). At the center of the X make a third hole and, again, do what you can with reinforcers or tape to prevent tearing.

Call the kite flyers together and explain phase two: procure tall grass, emphasis on *tall*. Think of wheat or oats— long, thick stems and tufted heads. Each piece of grass should be at least five inches longer than one diagonal of the X, so that it may act as both frame and tail for the kite. You may need all the troops to work on this phase. Tell them this is the essence of the kite. Without their resourceful contributions, there may be no kite. (Brooks—you remember Brooks, who went to buy the reinforcers, string, and tape—has made kites before and appreciates the absolute necessity of long grass. Walking back from the corner store provided an opportunity to reconnoiter . . . surely the municipal mowers weren't ruinously thorough?) Oh dear, no one seems to know where to find long grass. Well, you *can* substitute drinking straws for the frame if you absolutely have to, in which case you will need to send a secondary detail back inside to find alternate tails (crepe paper streamers, old holiday ribbon, strips of newspaper twisted into a series of bows, whatever is on hand that can be attached to the two bottom corners). If your tails are not extensions of the frame, they can be as much as seven times as long as the diagonal of the frame. Here's a little secret tightly held by veteran kite flyers: the perfect length for a tail is actually determined by sending the kite up and seeing how well it flies. If the tail is too short, the kite will dance around like a three-year-old filly at the starting gate. If the tail is too long, it will hang straight down—a millstone weighing down your fancies of flight.

Frames and tails procured, you can complete the assembly. Using a piece of kite string (baling twine is really too heavy and fishing line too hard to tie), lash two stems or straws

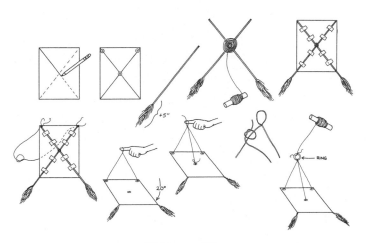

Making a Kite

together in such a way as to match the angles of the **X** on the back of the kite. This is done by alternating a series of figure eights or hourglass designs. Former campers may recall the oft-practiced God's-eye craft project—same-oh, same-oh. (If you have some good glue and several days to make your kite, you can slap some glue onto the center point of the lashing for additional strength, but only if time permits.) Next, tape or glue the frame to the kite. Go ahead, use plenty of tape, the more secure the better.

Now for the bridle. Through the two top holes, tie one end of a 20" piece of string to the frame. Make a loop (using the end-over-end first step in tying your shoe) in the middle of the string, and then, keeping the loop open and loose, tie the other end to the corresponding point on the frame (see the illustration). This will give you two "legs" of the bridle, with a loop in the middle. To determine the center point of the kite (which you hope is just over the cross-piece), put your finger in the loop (so that it won't close) and lift the kite off the floor. Is it balanced? Whew! But balance isn't everything in flying. You need to set the optimal angle of this aeronautical masterpiece. While keeping your finger inside the loop, allow the tail end to drop about twenty degrees. The third leg of the bridle, which is attached to the crosspiece and threaded through the center hole, should be brought up to meet the other two legs at that point. Mark the third string, and before you thread it through the carefully held loop, use it to make a second loop around the string that forms the first two legs (this is known as a fisherman's knot and it should hold in a light wind—you could have used a surgeon's knot, but Pat's still not back from the hospital). Pull the two loops in such a way as to meet the mark on the third leg of the bridle. The likelihood of anyone having a rivet or a little plastic curtain ring collecting lint at the bottom of a pocket is remote, but it's worth asking. In the absence of perfection, a small circle of string can easily be fashioned and tied to the point where the three legs meet. Why do you need a ring? Well, the bridle has a tendency to twist about and get fouled up with the line you are using to get the blasted kite up in the air. If the line is attached to a ring—rather than directly to the bridle—there is less chance for annoying entanglements.

Time to head outside and down to the park (or any other large, open, treeless, power-line-free space available). Don't forget to bring the gliders along. Ask if anyone knows which way the wind is blowing. (HINT: Look at the leaves on the trees, look at the movement of the clouds, look at the flight pattern of the sparrows or the flags on the plaza; stick your finger in your mouth, take it out, hold it up in the air: which side dried faster?) Again, these kites are best in a breeze and no match for a gale.

Everybody ready for the big moment? Start running into the wind, holding the kite up and out on a foot or two of string. As it starts to tug, let it have more line. (Kite string usually comes on a cardboard spool, with holes at the top and bottom. Slide a stick through those holes for a smooth release of string; it's easier than using your index fingers as a roller.) Don't give the kite too much line at once, otherwise it can rise above the upward draft it is riding and crash. Keep the line tight, releasing a yard at a time, until the kite is high overhead and appears to be in a steady flight pattern. That's it. Now's the time to hand it over to one of the younger kite-makers. After all, it's no fun to make a kite and then not be allowed to fly it. So it's flying, and you're all as high as, well, as high as those proverbial kites. Brooks is reminiscing about a kite he and his father put together long, long ago. "It was a galleon ship, a three-masted rig, made of parchment and balsa—two hundred and some-odd pieces in all—it took us the better part of a winter. We had real mixed feelings the day we launched her." Sandy and several of the children are taking advantage of the changing wind currents, performing loop-de-loops with their gliders. And here comes Pat, lab coat flapping as she hurries across the park. She swears she saw the kite, a dancing speck of white, from the fifth floor of the hospital, a signal to come out and play. "Three cheers for aerodynamics, ice-cream cones are on me." What a great afternoon.

Organizing a Scavenger Hunt and a Treasure Hunt

What is it about the human condition that prompts a perfectly balanced, seemingly normal person to drop twenty handwritten invitations into the mailbox? Is it a sense of duty, an act of boredom, or sheer madness? Perhaps the answer to why has something to do with who and how. A host who has earned the "life of his party" reputation just wants to spend Saturday night with friends. A hostess who is admired for her attention to infinitesimal details feels compelled to give the neighborhood's first luau. So, it boils down to personality. Consider the story of Mary and Martha. Jesus comes to visit his two good friends. Mary immediately abandons her household duties, preferring to sit and absorb His every word; Martha continues to bustle about, chopping and mixing the makings of a suitable feast. Mary's engaged in conversation and Martha "can't hear when the water's running." Who is the better hostess? Debate has continued through the ages—generally after the last good night and before the first good morning.

Of course, the answer is moot when you've invited perfect guests who can entertain themselves—and each other—while you worry over that "foolproof" chocolate soufflé. But what to do with the shy, retiring, Portuguese-speaking clutch of visiting in-laws whose host responded immediately to your invitation? (They're the ones in the far corner of the living room waiting for you to emerge from the kitchen.) Whether you are Mary or Martha, George or Harry, consider preparing an icebreaker to hold in reserve, especially if this is a solo stint as host.

If you identify with Martha, you might find merit in a scavenger hunt, which requires little more from the host than a firsthand knowledge of the environs—the house, the neighborhood, the island—and a few preparty preparations.

If there are places where trespassing is forbidden or snooping might be dangerous, they should be pointed out repeatedly before the hunt begins—"Don't go near the cliffs at the north end of the island . . ." or "As long as the chain-link fence is between you and the guard dogs . . ." or "That's where we keep Aunt Edna's porcelain collection, and since there is no porcelain on the list . . ."

Now, all you need to prepare is a list of ten or fifteen indigenous items. Consider the ages of your players and adjust the difficulty accordingly. At the top of the list there should be a general rule about taking things *By Permission Only*. Retrieving larkspur from Will Allbright's flower garden without his signature is as egregious as swiping the molasses crinkle cookie from the ceramic pig without Nanny Peco's initials. Of course, you will have to alert those neighbors most likely to be raided. Nanny Peco is the last of the big-time bakers (a fact these kids continue to bring to their parents' attention) and Will's larkspur reaches well over your fence . . . pretty hard to miss. (Of course, if you are a Martha you've already covered that—Will and Nancy are invited to join the party as soon as the twelfth scavenger has raced through.)

So, the list, with its warnings, could read: larkspur (one stem), a molasses crinkle cookie, a nickel, a marble, a bird's feather, a piece of red yarn, a murder mystery, and so on.

Items are listed in the first column and corresponding "borrowed from" blanks form the second. Each player gets a copy of the list and a bag. You know where all these things can be found, and if the players are half as observant as you, they should soon be back on your porch with a bag full of treasure *and* a certified list of borrowed goods.

Before the hunt begins, ask if there are any questions (Is a *dime* acceptable? Could the feather be from a budgie's tail?), so that guidelines are established in everyone's mind and the heartbreak of disallowed booty is kept to a minimum. As soon as the hunt begins, you will have successfully scattered the guests in a flurry of entertainment and given yourself all the time needed for the *gougères*—plus the potential for enough larkspur to fill out the centerpiece and cookies to serve with the berries—all without the slightest sense of missing out on the fun.

For Marys: the treasure hunt. This game involves considerably more preparation than a scavenger hunt; it also works best when there is some light-handed supervision, just to be sure the intended sequence is the one followed (by sheer "luck," a gang can jump from clue #1 to clue #15 and find the treasure in record time, providing a terrific opportunity to moralize on the consequences of pursuing instant gratification, but what fun is that?). It also may turn out that the site for clue #4 is to be revisited as the location of the treasure (you may have to lug the chest into place as soon as the unsuspecting group has moved on to clue #5). So there is a bit of overseeing to be done during the hunt, which shouldn't bother anyone who was going to play anyway.

Pictorial clues accommodate all ages. If you are a confirmed nonartist, you can resort to clipping facsimiles from discarded magazines. Only one copy of each clue is needed, as they are read at the site and left in place for those who have stopped to assess a skinned knee or marvel at the Jeffersonian brickwork in Will's garden. The first clue is shown to the group by the host (perhaps it's a picture of a red wagon). As soon as everyone has taken a good look at it, you release the pack, which will charge toward their individual (and sometimes collective) best guess as to where they will find a red wagon. Clue #2, found in said wagon, is a picture of a bookshelf draped by a Christmas cactus. Onward, but to the library? The upstairs hallway? Where is a bookcase with a flowerpot? And thus the group becomes dispersed and you do what you can to give additional hints to those who are least likely to find clue #3 (because it's much too early for them to get lost). Each clue leads to another, until the final clue uncovers the treasure—which, depending on the crowd, may be favorite popsicle flavors or an impressive variety of microbrews.

If the prize is the latter, all self-respecting, legal-aged beer drinkers should be expected to use those brain cells before destroying them. Instead of relying on pictures or cartoons for the clues, try to present each one in riddle form or as a rhyming cryptogram. The locations could be chosen and described using a selection of poems—"Something there is that doesn't love a _____" or "I have eaten the plums that were in the _____." Perhaps lyrics from the golden oldies, geographic directions (with the exact number of paces and five-and-dime compasses), or foreign (even dead) languages would be more appropriate for your party. Whatever you decide to do, remember that the object is to build a team along the way to finding that well-earned reward. Mary's fun is in the weeklong search for hiding places and literary lines, to say nothing of listening to her guests' wild guesses and watching their competitive natures meld and mellow. Everyone wins a prize at the end, and the group's conversation, otherwise predictable repeats of what has fallen from the mouths of bosses and babes, has a new focus. Dinner preparations? Wasn't it potluck?

Whistling

"You know how to whistle, don't you?" asks the sultry Bacall. And Bogart flashes that sheepish-while-flabbergasted grin.

There are whistles, and there are whistles. Short and shrill for dogs, long and modulated for victory, salacious for legs, piercing for cabs. Each and every one of them is made to gain attention, and for every person who can "just put his lips together and blow," there are fourteen who say they can't. No one's quite sure when they last tried, but for reasons that remain unclear, the inability to whistle (or to snap fingers or wiggle ears) has become an acceptable shortcoming. In some circles, whistling is completely dismissed — rowdy behavior bespeaking questionable lineage, a perception that may have more to do with sour grapes than politesse. Perhaps if whistling were presented as a gentle amusement to pass the evening hours it would make a comeback.

Begin with some subtle assistance, in this case a wide piece of grass long enough to run from the top of your thumb to the base of your hand. Stretch the blade along the outside edge of one thumb and hold it in place with the outside edge of the other. Thumbs parallel? Good. Now bend them slightly, at the second joint, and rest your lips on the knuckles. Start blowing, not hard and not all at once, but in a slow, steady manner. Inhale and try again. (It might be helpful to get a brown paper lunch bag or a wax paper sandwich bag to breathe into should hyperventilation bring on the dizzies. It happens to every beginner, so you may as well know the remedy and keep the progress smooth.) Back to the whistle. Make sure the grass is taut. At some point the blade will begin to make a squeaky sound, which means you are definitely on the right track. Keep blowing and eventually you will produce a shrill, high-pitched tone. With further experimentation, you will be able to redirect the flow of air and vary the pitch.

Once you have mastered the blade of grass whistle, there's every reason to give the dove call a whirl. Thumbs are held together in the same position used for the blade of grass whistle, but your hands are cupped together and the blade of grass has been dropped. The pad of the left thumb rests between the base and first knuckle of the left index finger, holding that finger perpendicular to the thumb. The mid-

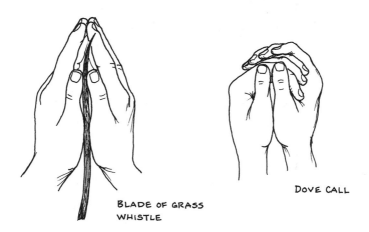

BLADE OF GRASS
WHISTLE

DOVE CALL

dle, ring, and little fingers are tiered over the top of the index finger. Open your right hand and move it toward your left one as if you were trying to make a cup to catch a refreshing sip of brook water. The right thumb fits alongside the left thumb, the bases and outside edges of the hands are tightly pressed together, and the four other right fingers are behind those of the left hand. Imagine you are trying to carry a secret fluid from one room to another, no leaks, and the only hole is between your thumbs' first and second knuckles. When you blow, blow across the hole made by your thumbs (if you blow into the hole you'll come up empty-handed). Having trouble? Maybe you need to stick the thumb knuckles out at more of an angle. Maybe you need to tighten up the chamber. Maybe you need to shake out your hands and start over. The sound you are going for is definitely birdlike in a hooting, cooing sort of way. After you have practiced holding your hands and bending your thumbs so that you can call the covey on the first try, play around with variations by fluttering the fingers on your right hand (maybe just the little finger and the ring finger). Of course, it takes practice, but when you've got the knack you're ready to go for a higher form of whistling—hailing a cab.

A whistle that commands is clearly the most impressive. It is also the most challenging to master. As far as anyone knows, it is impossible only for those who never really give it a try. Convinced? Good. The idea behind the whistle is to force a steady flow of air through a small opening, whether it is formed by two fingers or the tip of your tongue. When hailing a cab, you may have your hands full, so if you can manage a whistle that relies only on the tongue, lips, and teeth, you won't have to drop your bags.

Stretch your lower lip tightly over your bottom teeth. Tighter. Lift your tongue ever so slightly (in time you'll know the position without giving it a second thought . . . in time) and try to shape it into a V. Wait a minute. Look in the mirror. Did you ever try to roll your tongue? Never? Well, put your little finger on the center of the tip of the tongue and push down as you pull the sides of the tongue up. Now, take your finger out and try without it. Your tongue's almost a V. Back to the tightly drawn bottom lip. While you are making a V with the tip of your tongue, pull your lower jaw back ever so slightly. Now smooth your upper lip over the top of your upper teeth and blow. Blow again. Relax. Breathe into the bag if you feel light-headed. Resume the position: lower lip tight across bottom teeth, tongue tip in a V, back of tongue raised slightly to pull tip back, and top lip sealing mouth along the top of upper teeth. Now blow. Keep trying. Tighten the lips, rearrange the tongue, blow again. You'll get it, and once you do, don't stop until you're sure you can find the very same position next time you're in a hurry to get across town.

NOTE: Practicing is encouraged throughout this book, as it is throughout life. Listening to one who is learning to whistle can be annoying, however (to those who have already mastered the art and to the majority who won't). Thus it's best to save rehearsals for an evening walk, a solo sail, or an empty apartment.

Juggling

Marshmallows have a universal appeal. They raise the level of energy for both the weary and the tireless. Bring them on a camping trip and they never fail to evoke memories— "Gee, the last time I roasted a marshmallow was when I . . ." —which may be all the entertainment the evening needs. But there is a better reason to make sure you have a bag of regulation-size marshmallows (no pastel minis, please), and that reason is empowerment. One bag—or maybe it should be an *extra* bag— can encourage an entire party to push the envelope of their humdrum, everyday lives; to clear away their self-imposed limitations; to realize untapped collective potential. In short, with one bag of marshmallows you can teach them to juggle.

Of course, you will have mastered this feat long before you tuck the bag of marshmallows into your backpack. And maybe you won't want to learn with marshmallows. You can start out with beanbags or tennis balls or three "sock" balls (made by holding two socks together at the toes, rolling them tightly toward the open ends, holding the roll and three of the four top edges in one hand, and peeling the fourth back and around the meet the other three—encasing the roll and forming a ball). Whatever you use, the three objects should be uniform in weight and size and not fragile . . . just in case they are dropped.

Start with the basics, tossing one ball from the right hand to the left hand and back again. It seems so rudimentary, so ridiculous, but keep tossing until the flow is steady and the ball follows an arc from the tossing hand to the catching hand. Juggling happens within that plane or it doesn't happen at all. So, la di da, there you stand, tossing one ball back and forth. Ten good catches for every one missed. Getting bored? Try doing this simple exercise with your eyes closed. If your elbows remain at waist level and the arc is not much higher than eye level, you should begin to hit the same ratio (ten catches to one drop). Time for a break (yawn, stretch, take out the trash, brush your teeth, put your mind on hold). Don't worry, this first session is enough to pique your curiosity. You won't give it up now.

It may be the next morning, it could be later the same evening, sooner or later you will be distracted by those same three balls sitting on top of your bookcase. Ten more minutes couldn't hurt. Reassure yourself that you have mastered the basic rhythm of toss and catch. Looks as if you're ready to add a second ball. Eyes opened wide, a ball in each hand, the first toss is made, and just as that ball is starting its descent, the second toss is made—not straight across, remember, but up into the same arc. One up, two up, one down, two down, the rhythm gets smoother with practice. It's okay to talk to yourself. Students of ballroom dancing whisper sequences, "slow, quick, quick"; jugglers name revolutions, "one, two, three," giving each ball the same amount of time (slow, slow, slow or quick, quick, quick—any variation at this stage will bring on disaster). Don't worry. It may take a little time to develop the knack. But once you do, you are on your way.

Time to add the third ball. Put it in the hand that works best for you. Do what you can to visualize the arc. If it helps, and only if it helps, draw one on the refrigerator or the sliding glass door (use lipstick, it comes off). Ready? Toss one of the two balls held in your right (or dominant) hand. Wait for it to head back down before tossing the ball up from your left hand. Watch the second ball reach the top of the arc as the first ball falls into your left hand, which should happen just as you toss the third ball up into the arc. Wow.

It almost worked the first time. And after about twenty minutes, it works almost every time.

Now you can start looking around for anything that comes in threes. A new awareness has taken hold and you see things differently. The epergne of fruit, the basket of dinner rolls, the collection of napkin rings . . . oh, the fun you can have. As you continue to polish your newfound pastime, experiment with a variety of shapes and weights. The laws of gravity scream out in protest. "Nonsense," you say with confidence, knowing that your brain can do calculations so quickly they seem to be intuitions. Yes, the egg is heavier than the Ping-Pong ball, and lighter than the orange, but (with practice) you'll regulate the timing of the throws to offset the differences.

This is more than satisfactory, this is fantastic. Which means it is time to share the wealth. Marshmallows, remember the marshmallows? You were getting ready to go to a cookout and you weren't going to arrive empty-handed. Nancy and R.J. are delighted to see you, and the kids are ecstatic. "She didn't bring wine, she brought MARSHMALLOWS!" Why try to explain by way of apology? It's so done. Launch into a demonstration instead. Open the bag and pull out three puffy cylinders. Inspect each one, testing for weight, size, and a sufficient amount of magic. To the children's confusion and their parents' relief, you tell them that these are for something much better than roasting and begin to juggle.

Why do you need a bag of fifty-four marshmallows if you are going to be using only three? Because one measure of true talent is inspiration. By the end of your show you'll need enough "balls" for an entire team of jugglers. And marshmallows are uniform as well as easy to see in the firelight; small hands can catch them; they are light to carry in; and they don't need to be carried out. The drop factor takes care of nutritional concerns—nobody wants to eat a marshmallow covered with dirt! Well, almost nobody. But your jugglers are well on their way to becoming major talents, emboldened, empowered, imbued by potential. Who would have thought all that could come from three lumps of fluff?

Telling a Story

Standing in a shower you didn't leave time enough to take, you decide to ignore the telephone. It stops ringing. The answering machine screens Marcia's frenzied plea: "Gerry, if you're there, pick up . . . I've got the sleeping bag, the food, the bug dope, but no car . . . and since we're both getting a late start . . ." Message ends, phone rings again. That will be Marcia, hoping her first try was a wrong number, you surmise, streaking from the shower to the phone only because (a) Marcia will continue to redial until you pick up and (b) there's bound to be a story waiting. Years ago you came up with the theory that Marcia's life is best understood as an endless string of vignettes. What you have yet to determine is how much of that is because of Marcia. Is she in fact an alien with a magnetic story-attracting core? Or is she only able to cope with life as fiction? Most of the time Marcia's stories are funny, about her childhood, her boss, her tag sales. Sometimes they are sad, although Marcia hates to make anyone cry—so she invariably throws a spin in at the end, O. Henry style. Occasionally they are too long (once she caught you dozing while she was tracing a princess's lineage through six generations of ineffective rulers). But always, always, you (and a host of friends) can count on Marcia for a story.

On the way over to pick her up—it's really only fifteen minutes out of the way—you have a chance to recall the last story you heard Marcia tell and to think more seriously about storytelling in general. For starters, most stories have a beginning, a middle, and an end, and the audience is meant to hear all three parts (unless it's after nine and the listener is under six). Well and good, but it doesn't begin to explain the universal fascination stories hold. Beyond the plot, there is the promise of being carried away from vexations, securely suspended by fantasy. A skilled storyteller not only maneuvers imaginations around interruptions and over inconsistencies, transforming breakfast nooks into banquet halls, pots of geraniums into rain forests; he convinces a group of people to travel to those secret, fabulous places without the use of slides or maps or souvenirs. But let's face it, it's Marcia's delivery that turns the weakest of stories into mesmerizing delights. It's her voice, conveying a full command of the emotional spectrum (combined with an uncanny feel for the audience), and her riveting eyes.

There she is, waiting curbside. You slow well ahead of where she is standing, knowing her frightening habit of jumping into moving vehicles. What looks like enough food and clothing for the Special Forces' next assignment is heaved into the back, and before the door can slam shut, she begins, "You'll never believe it . . . ," all in one long sigh, eyes rolling toward the car roof. "But you have to promise not to tell a soul," and you are securely locked into her confidence. It works like a charm.

How are your storytelling skills? You've never thought to ask yourself? Try this: stand in front of a mirror and describe the face of a thoroughly threatening villain: the hair, the ears, the nose, the chin. Having trouble? Who do you know that fits the description? You don't? Then think of Long John Silver, or Cinderella's evil stepmother. There you go. Deliver the description and then step back and analyze it. What moved? The line of your brow, the lid of one eye, the side of your mouth? How did you sound? Did you pause, cackle, whisper, sigh? So much potential, and that's before you've even started to think of the story line. Marcia has an uncanny knack for turning the mundane into the most fantastic and often unpredictable stories. She lives for material. And maybe that's why she's never at a loss for a story. But you tend to see things not as they might be but as they are. If it weren't for Marcia, you would probably support the notion that there are really only so many story lines, probably no more than eight or nine. New stories are old stories with additional complexities. Pygmalion is reborn in *My Fair Lady*, Romeo and Juliet belong to rival gangs in *West Side Story*. Aesop's fables, Grimms' fairy tales, Greek and Roman myths are all beautifully bound and available in most bookstores. But no one tells those stories after dinner. At least Marcia doesn't. Her tales are always so fresh, so relevant.

"So *there* I was, on the side of the road, with a car *full* of camping supplies. Did you see the list Amy sent out? I couldn't *believe* it, the details were almost discouraging. I mean, a jackknife I have, but she wasn't listing just any jackknife, Gerry, Amy wants you to have a jackknife with a can opener, scissors, and an awl. Did she go on one of those wilderness programs when she was younger? Anyway, there I was, in plenty of time to make the Exit 8 rendezvous, when my car decided to slow from a left-lane sprint to a breakdown-lane crawl. No reason, no flashing signal, no weird noise, just a total loss of forward motion. I'm thinking about the melting ice packs, the vanishing time, and the red Volvo on my right (which is interpreting my gestures to move over and let this ailing car of mine off the roadway to mean 'HEY, want to drag?'), and when the tow truck finally pulls up, I'm wondering, why don't I have a car phone? A triple-A card? Plain old dumb luck? Some combination of the three? So I don't notice that the driver is standing there, chain and hook in hand, not moving or anything, just staring at me." Which is what Marcia is doing to you. Try to keep your eyes on the road while she comes to the end of the saga.

It's going to be a late night and Marcia's had a busy week, of course you don't mind if she takes a little nap. The campsite is under an hour away and you feel wide awake after hearing about the deranged service man who thought Marcia was his long-lost sister. Picking up the threads of an earlier rumination, you draw up a critique of her latest performance.

She didn't use many gestures, but she did give the man a slight accent and an attitude through her tone of voice. Her observations were completely subjective (that man gave her the absolute *creeps!*). And when she was describing a scene or a face, it was as if she were seeing them again. The weather wasn't just dark and stormy, it was becoming wild with wind pushing black clouds toward the south. Your day was spent cooped up in a windowless office, no clues of a foreboding sky, but still you had no trouble imagining the oncoming storm as she looked up with a frown toward the heavens. While you concentrated on your driving, you could feel her eyes. They never left you. Her pace mirrored the action in the story. Slowing as the car slowed, stopping with the realization that the service man was staring, racing as she described getting into the cab of his truck. There are so many elements involved, and they are so deceptively simple, basic, natural. Marcia's art is knowing just when to use them, and how.

Her magic is knowing which story is the best one to tell. On another camping trip, after a day of fishing, she told a fantastic story about a young man who decided to abandon his plans to read for the law and made it his goal to cast a fly in every stream north of the 45th parallel . . . and about the striking blonde woman he met on her return from the very same adventure. Another time, after a heavy existential dinner conversation, she came up with a gentle, lyrical tale about a search for the golden coins of a lost civilization. Coins, so the legend goes, which, when held, transform into bubbles floating visions of life's joys. It was inspired.

Marcia wakes up, stretches, and asks how much longer. She begins talking about Jack—"His tent will be up before the rest of us have unpacked our stakes"—and Amy's beau, Steve, who planned the weekend's menu—"He'll be measuring out portions of freeze-drieds for tonight's feed." What started as a review of the guest list becomes a critique of an overly serious few. They're the ones who will be comparing state-of-the-art equipment and stamina-building fitness machines well after everyone else is zipped in for the night. It's an attitude that flies in the face of Marcia's casual appreciation for the out-of-doors. Then a slow smile begins to spread across her face. Her eyes widen and begin to sparkle. She's just remembered an absolutely terrifying ghost story about three gung-ho types who have to hole up in a cave together to wait out two days of treacherous weather.

Finding a Constellation

It's the end of a good day, maybe even an extraordinary day. You walked along the path to the cove. Parents made lively conversation. Children flew kites against a brilliant blue sky and splashed in the water as it came in across the warm sand. The only noises were from birds and waves, and there was just enough of a breeze to keep the mosquitoes at bay. The food that was pulled from baskets and packs was better than anything anyone could remember eating. How long had it been since you'd given in to the temptation of a deviled egg? It was a day to savor, and as the sun sinks into the horizon, no one wants to leave this last bit of summer. Why should they? Everyone brought sweaters, Nick has promised to carry Max when his legs get too tired, and anyway, how often do you get to see the stars? The night sky without the light of the city?

Lying on your back, resting your head in your hands, you look up and for the first time in years remember the mobile of the Sun Family your mother helped you construct out of papier-mâché molded over balloons. The biggest one was the sun; hanging from that was a wad for Mercury, connected to a slightly larger Venus, followed by Earth, a red ball for Mars, then a sizable Jupiter and fancy Saturn with a paper-plate ring. You know there were more planets, but it's been a long time since you put that mobile up in the attic. There was a later encounter with astronomy in college, when you were fulfilling a science requirement for English majors with a semester of Rocks and Stars. Identifying constellations was just part of a midterm, and you couldn't remember one now if you had to.

Well, maybe one. Everyone knows the Big Dipper. It's the one with seven stars, four to shape the straight-sided cup of the ladle and three more to make its long handle. Sometimes it appears to be upside down or standing on end. The autumn sky, at least in the northern United States and Canada, shows it most like a dipper that *isn't* spilling water. "How do

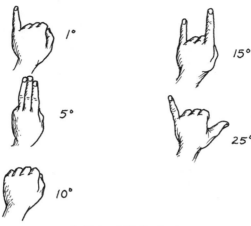

A Makeshift Sextant

you know that's the Big Dipper?" asks Max, who has caught a second wind. Resist the standard "because I do" reply; after all, someone once did the same for you. So how do you know? And how did anyone who used the stars for navigation hundreds of years ago know this?

"Here you go, Max, hold up your hand." You proceed to show Max, and a growing number of others, how the hand (young, old, large, small . . . any hand) can be used as a makeshift sextant. One degree is roughly the width of your little finger (stretch your arm out and hold up a fist, extend the little finger only). Open your fist, hold the little finger down with your thumb, and the three upright middle fin-

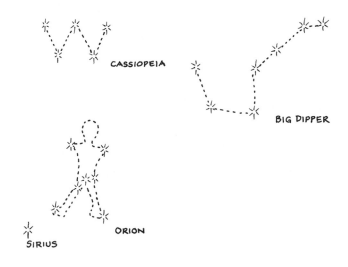

gers will represent five degrees. Ten degrees is the width of your fist, fifteen is between the little finger (slightly extended) and the index finger, and twenty-five degrees is between the tip of the little finger (still extended) and the outstretched thumb (as if you were reaching for the piano key above an octave). The rim of the Big Dipper's cup is approximately ten degrees across. (Don't worry, there isn't that much math to this; once you've gone to this much trouble to find the Big Dipper you won't have to do it again.) If you think you've spotted the constellation and want to check, put your fist up and see if it fits. The depth of the cup is five degrees, or three fingers' width. The length from the end of the handle to the tip of the lip is just over twenty-five degrees. So, there, you've proved it is the Big Dipper.

"Find another one for me," says the adoring Max, and you can't bear to let him down. Look for Cassiopeia, a W-shaped constellation of five stars. In the winter sky you'll find her by drawing a line from the Big Dipper's handle (actually, the third star from the end of the handle) to the tip of the Little Dipper's handle — it's roughly fifty degrees off to the west. Now extend the line another fifty degrees and you've reached the middle of Cassiopeia's W.

"Who's Cassiopeia?" asks Max's older sister. Well, mythically speaking, she was the proud queen of King Cepheus. Now it seems that this mortal queen's excessive vanity led her to unwisely compare herself to the gods. When the sea nymphs heard that Cassiopeia thought she ranked above them on the beauty charts, they enlisted the aid of a menacing sea monster to ravage the coastline of Cepheus's kingdom. The only acceptable truce involved the sacrifice of the royal daughter, Princess Andromeda, who was to be chained to a rock for the sea monster's dinner. Poor King Cepheus. Poorer still, Princess Andromeda. As luck would have it, young Perseus happened to be flying by (he had wings on his sandals). He slew the monster (he had a magic sword), rescued the girl, and declared she would become his bride.

Then all Hades broke loose. In order to stop the madness, Perseus was forced to empty his bag of tricks, producing the snaky head of a Gorgon girl (Medusa, to her friends). One look at her and the raging mob became stone silent—that is, silent stones. The downside: both Cassiopeia and Cepheus were in the mob. The upside: to make up for her untimely demise, the gods granted Cassiopeia a place in the heavens. Even the sea nymphs agreed she could be there (on the condition that half the time her crown would be upside down as a sign of her newfound humility).

Just below Cassiopeia's constellation is a fuzzy bit of light. That's her daughter, Andromeda, whose name claims a cluster of stars bigger than the Milky Way (the big path of starlight mere mortals see going all the way across the sky on a very clear night). It looks like a small blur because it is so far away. In fact, the light from Andromeda took about two million years to get to us. So go ahead, ask your mom and dad, is Andromeda still there or is she just a twinkle in Cassiopeia's eye?

And there is the mighty hunter Orion, brightest constellation of the winter sky. The left shoulder is orange-red Betelgeuse, his right foot is Rigel, and three stars in a diagonal form his belt (the easiest way to pick out this constellation). If you are having trouble finding Orion, go back to the Big Dipper. Using the star that marks the lip of the cup, count off fifty degrees (two hand spans) in an overhead direction. One, two . . . now you are touching Capella. Keep following the overhead path for another forty-five degrees (almost two hand spans) and you should be marking Orion's belt.

And who was Orion? He was none other than the son of Poseidon, and a very big son at that. In fact, he was so tall that when he wanted to go from one Greek island to another, he could walk along the ocean floor without getting his head wet. And he was such a fierce hunter that when the people of nearby Chios were completely overwhelmed by vicious lions and frenzied wolves, Orion and his dog, Sirius, restored order in an afternoon. Now, you might want to know what became of Orion and his trusty pal. This handsome giant's hunting prowess was eventually noticed by Artemis, the goddess of the moon—in short, she took a shine to him. Predictably, her attentions inflated Orion's oversized ego and he became a man obsessed. "I won't sleep until I have the heads of all the animals in Greece mounted on the walls of my lodge," he declared. Well, a small scorpion overheard all this talk and felt the safety of his kingdom was at risk. (At this point you can explain about scorpions, their claws and poisonous curling tail.) So he did what every brave soldier would do: he lay awake all night waiting for Orion to come back to his island home for a nap, and then he gave him everything he had. The gods were saddened by Orion's death, even though a few dismissed it as just another case of hubris with a twist. But the majority prevailed and Orion was put in the heavens, with Sirius at his feet (twenty degrees southeast from the end of Orion's belt). The gods also recognized the bravery of the scorpion who had saved the wild animals from becoming mere trophies, and so the scorpion is also in the sky. Now the gods are clever, and they suspect that some wounds never heal: to avoid further rifts, Orion leaves the sky just as the scorpion is rising.

"You mean they don't have to share?" asks Max, baiting his mother, who always insists that everyone *must.* But she doesn't rise to his teasing. She's lost in the stars, recalling a night long before Max was even a notion. She was seventeen, chosen above two seniors to play Juliet in the spring production. She smiles at Max from light-years away and quietly begins:

> Come gentle night; come, loving, black-browed night;
> Give me my Romeo; and, when I shall die,
> Take him and cut him out in little stars,
> And he will make the face of heaven so fine
> That all the world will be in love with night
> And pay no worship to the garish sun.

My, my. It's positively amazing what a little stargazing can do. In a minute or so it will be time to gather up the blankets and baskets for the trip home . . . to sleep, perchance to dream . . . of gods and mortals and the starry sky.

Further Possibilities for the Weekend

... A PERFECT GUEST DEPARTS

❖

When it comes to saying good night, there are basically three types of guests: those who need to leave, those who know when to leave, and those who will have to be thrown out. Members of the third group are, for the most part, only a temporary bother: these are the natural-born stay-at-homes who have yet to find a life partner or a permanent address. Today's last-to-leave is tomorrow's early-to-bed. While every party has one or two of these hangers-on, they are excused. It's a brief stage in an otherwise long and quiet life.

The second group, those who know when to leave, will help those who don't. You can count on it. These are the punctual, the practical, the polite beyond simple manners. They are good friends who have work to go to in the morning or who must consider the baby-sitter, whose meter is still running. Their lives mirror yours. Often they share space with you—in the office, on the court—and over time they have come to appreciate nuances of style.

After a delicious dinner and heartfelt conversation, Harriet realizes the time. It is late. Not LATE, but definitely time to go. The food has been consumed, the presents have been opened, the coffee has been drained; whatever the demands of the occasion—they've been met. Now is the time to bid adieu, now, as the tenor begins to slip: hearty laughter fades to sighs; eyes once bright in anticipation are dull; voices are softer and minds slower. It's a natural lull—the signal to depart. There are other lulls, to be sure, unnatural ones, which often occur in the early, awkward moments of a party: the *hostess* knows everyone and she's sure they'll like each other, once they get past the introductions. These painful, inevitable silences are sometimes made worse by the well-intentioned guest who feels the need to finish another's sentence or by the two who ask the same question simultaneously ("Isn't this a lovely house?") and then wonder if they are in an echo chamber or mysteriously linked by ESP. For this very reason, Marcia (known for her wild stories) and Pete (an erstwhile magician) are always invited to parties. They read these pregnant pauses as a signal to rally, not to leave. And, indeed, no one did leave this evening. At least until now, when it is "time."

There are as many farewell techniques as stars in the sky. Harriet exercises subtle body language (shoulders begin to slump as head turns toward husband, legs uncross, feet lower to the floor, hands slide from lap to knees . . . it's just enough to get Buddy's attention). She gives her husband the old glance-to-the-wrist (watch or no watch) while raising both eyebrows. Now, Buddy is no fool. He may have missed these signals when they were first married, but after a number of awareness sessions in the car on the way home, he's able to read them "loud and clear."

And he's not alone. Jean starts in again on how much she has eaten, especially that second sliver of Derby pie, and what makes her think she'll ever wear a size four again? "But we can't leave you with all these dishes to clean up!" She rises to tidy up and is instantly followed by one or two others. The hosts can accept or dismiss the kindness, it's up to them. Maybe there's a dishwasher, a housekeeper, or they are unfazed by a sink full of dirty dishes the morning after and are just dying to hit the hay. It could be that party postmortems have become a favorite private moment. Whatever the decision, it was an offer made by way of saying, "It's time to think about leaving."

Now there is a commotion to get coats from the upstairs bedroom (another cue for the few in group number three). While they are being retrieved, it is up to you to summarize in ten words or less just what it was that made this party truly memorable. Was it the charming new couple? The plans for a business venture? The game of charades? (HINT: It should have something to do with the host's effort.) And with those ten words, steady eye contact, a firm handshake or a buzz on the cheek, you are out the door. You are out the door, into your car, and down the driveway. No lengthy good-byes along the walkway (you may be sporting a wool overcoat, but your host is shivering in shirtsleeves). No last-minute plans for tomorrow's game. "We'll call in the morning. Thanks again." Remember, you may have started the exodus, but your hostess has ten more guests who are waiting to be packed off and she really can't afford to heat all of the outdoors in the process.

And just what if those remaining guests were expecting to stay a bit longer? And what if your host was hoping for the same? (After all, dinner wasn't served until eight). This is the predicament of the guest who falls into the first cluster: "I wouldn't miss dinner with you and Henry for all the world, but I must warn you, my mother's plane arrives at ten after ten that same night and I've promised to meet it, so I'm afraid I'll have to slip out a little early. Is that all right?" Well, of course it is. You are the life of the party, and everyone is anxious to hear about your trip to Bali with the Round-Up Boys. Regardless of the party's pace, you are responsible for seeing yourself out at the prearranged time. But not before finding an opportunity to apologize to the general assembly for your early departure (encourage them to continue the merrymaking—you'll be there in spirit) and to pay tribute to the hosts . . . "Please don't get up."

"Good night," you say. The host and hostess turn and thank you for coming. "It wouldn't be a party without you,

you know." She repeats your punch line as you shake hands and turn down the path leading to a string of frost-covered cars. Wasn't that great? The food was tasty, the wine was interesting, old friends were in good form, and you were really quite taken by the new friends just made. Those two can really give a party.

The car turns over (amazing), and while you wait for the heater to rally you think about the difference between the function you went to last week (a real dud) and tonight's gathering. It has to do with who did what. Even though the caterer was renowned and the music was live, last week's guests acted as if they were in isolation booths. Tonight everyone was a part of the show. Yes, you did tell a very funny joke (remember to thank Jim) and, true to form, Alex carried the group over the after-dinner hump with an exceptional trick. You had no idea Charlotte and Henry would want to play charades, or that they would be so damned good. No wonder it's after midnight. You hope you didn't keep the Haddens up too late. But they were the ones to ask for another round of titles. All in all, a very good night.